# The Actor's Art and Craft

Other titles by Rona Laurie:

*Auditioning: A Practical Guide for Drama Students*
*Festivals and Adjudication*
*A Hundred Speeches from the Theatre*
*Scenes and Ideas*

# The Actor's Art and Craft

## Rona Laurie

*F.G.S.M., L.R.A.M., G.O.D.A., F.R.S.A.*

*Director of the Teachers' Licentiate and Chairman of the Drama
Advisory Board of the Guildhall School of Music and Drama*

## J. Garnet Miller Limited

Copyright © 1994 by Rona Laurie

First published in 1994 by
**J. Garnet Miller Limited**
*(A division of Cressrelles Publishing Company Limited)*
10 Station Road Industrial Estate, Colwall,
Near Malvern, Worcestershire WR13 6RN.

British Library Cataloguing in Publication Data:

Laurie, Rona
Actor's Art and Craft
I. Title
792.028

ISBN: 0-85343-595-2

Printed and bound in Great Britain by
BPC Wheatons Ltd, Exeter

# Contents

# Illustrations

# Chapter One

## How It All Began

"Good my Lord, will you see the players well bestowed?
Do you hear, let them be well used; for they are the
abstracts and brief chronicles of the time."
*Hamlet*

I am lying on the dusty stage of the Temperance Hall, Derby. I am ten years old and playing the part of Moth in an amateur production of *A Midsummer Night's Dream*. My costume consists of two layers of chiffon - one grey and one silvery blue, cut in handkerchief points around the hem. The stage is moonlit and I can see a dim glow of footlights and beyond them, stretching back into space, rows and rows of blurred faces. I am suddenly aware that this is the place where I want to be and I know with complete certainty that the theatre is going to be my life. And the theatre has indeed become its

1

focal point. I never had any wish for fame (which is just as well, because it has never come) but I have always been involved in some aspect of the theatre, whether acting, directing, coaching actors or writing about matters theatrical.

The urge to write this particular book came to me whilst I was sitting in Wembley Arena watching the World Ice-Skating Champions, Jayne Torvill and Christopher Dean, during their first professional tour. They enthralled their vast audience. It was the apparent ease of their performance, which came from a complete mastery of technique, their perfect timing and economy of movement and, above all, their ability to communicate everything which they were doing, which captured everybody. I looked round at the rows and rows of rapt faces. But of course, I thought, these are the self-same qualities which an actor needs. It is not an original idea, I admit, and would seem to be so obvious as not to need saying. And then I considered the thousands of words which are poured out every day about the art of acting on radio and television programmes, in the columns of newspapers, in interviews, in books and magazines, and the comparatively few which are devoted to the actor's craft. Perhaps now is the time, I thought, to re-state some of the old truths and, at the same time, try to expose some fallacies.

## Some Fallacies

By far the most common and persistent of these fallacies is the idea that an actor may have technique or he may have feeling, but he cannot have both at the same time. I have often heard American students say that American actors have depth of emotion whereas English actors are merely technical (the use of the word "merely" is significant). This is to wholly misunderstand the function of technique and its relation to feeling. Rather than inhibiting it, a mastery of technique frees the actor's emotion and is the means by which he can communicate it to an audience.

Placido Domingo, the great tenor, once said that he didn't have to think of his singing at all in the role of Othello but could concentrate on acting the part and conveying its passion. He was on top of the technique. Technique is the hand-maiden of feeling and not a deadening disciplinarian.

There will usually be a moment in rehearsal when an actor will create spontaneously the exact imaginative response to a situation in the play. His feeling will be true. He then has to remember how he felt at that moment and use his technique to reproduce this emotion so that even during a matinée, with a dull audience, when he is feeling completely uninspired, his performance will never fall below a certain level. A conductor was once asked whether he would prefer to conduct a brilliant amateur orchestra or a run-of-the-mill professional one. He replied,

"The professional one every time, the amateur orchestra may give some outstandingly good performances but will also give some very bad ones. I can rely on the professional, never to fall below a certain standard."

Consistency is the result of mastery of technique and argues a sense of responsibility towards an audience. An actor, particularly during a long run of a play, cannot always rely on inspiration and a spontaneous flow of emotion.

Some actors, it is true, are able to release emotion easily, but they have not acquired the technique to communicate it to their audience. In his book *Early Stages*, John Gielgud says,

"I nearly always enjoyed acting the last two scenes of the play (*Richard of Bordeaux*). I had found a way of playing these scenes in complete control of my own emotions, although the audience became more and more affected, to the point of tears."

Through a mastery of technique he was able to communicate his feeling more effectively.

I was once taken to task at an Amateur Drama Festival for saying in my adjudication that more emotion was needed from the actress playing the leading part. "But," she said when I met her afterwards, "I felt it all *here* (striking her bosom)." That was the trouble - the emotion was all locked inside her instead of being conveyed to the audience.

A second fallacy, perhaps not so widespread as the first, is that improvisation can do all that is necessary to prepare an actor for the performance of a part. Few people doubt the value of improvisation in freeing an actor from inhibitions, in developing his powers of imagination and emotional response, in helping him to explore a character and situation. However, I was wholeheartedly in agreement with Peter Hall when he said,

"People have concentrated too much recently on improvisation, which is basically a means of freshening-up the actor. It is time we got back to the craft of acting."

There seems to be a curious reluctance on the part of some directors to get down to the nitty-gritty of the text. One hears of six-week rehearsal periods of which the first three are devoted to improvisation exercises. The results are all too apparent in postponed or under-rehearsed first nights when the actors are not only shaky on their lines but seem unable to cope with the complexities of the dialogue. False emphases abound and even inconsistencies in the pronunciation of proper names. Plays by Chekov suffer particularly in this last respect.

A third fallacy and, I believe, one which is becoming more widespread is - it would have been better if Shakespeare had not written in verse. And so attempts are made to disguise the fact that the plays are written in blank verse. It seems strange that the language of our greatest dramatic poet is so often treated in this cavalier fashion. The trouble starts in school, unless the pupils are fortunate enough to have an enlightened and imaginative member of staff teaching them English and/or Drama. In this case, a Shakespeare play will be treated as something to be spoken aloud, to be acted, to be discussed. Too often, however, the excitement and splendour of the verse will be lost in a welter of footnotes and academic analysis of exam-orientated themes. This approach may be continued in further education.

When I was running a post-graduate course in Elizabethan and Jacobean theatre, I was astonished to find that not one of the graduates, some of whom came from university Drama Departments, was capable of reading the blank verse expressively. It transpired that they had never been encouraged to read Shakespeare aloud either at school or university, although nearly all had improvised on the themes and plots of the plays.

Too many drama teachers and tutors use Shakespeare merely as a source of material for improvisation. This is, of course, a useful way of exploring character and plot but the principal value of these exercises is discovered when they lead on to the actual text.

Too much is made of the difficulties of Shakespeare's language and prosody. The iambic metre is the nearest one to the pattern of everyday speech. We all, at some time must have unconsciously spoken a line of regular blank verse, for example,

⏑ — ⏑ — ⏑ — ⏑ — ⏑ —

"The train / from In / verness / is ov / erdue."
(with apologies to British Rail)

And then there is also the famous story of Sarah Siddons reprimanding a servant at Sir Walter Scott's dinner-table in the tones of Lady Macbeth,

"I ordered water, boy, you've brought me beer."

A line of regular iambic metre. I am often surprised at how well a drama student who has never before read Shakespeare aloud will instinctively respond to the metre and rhythm of the lines.

Now that I've got rid of those troublesome bees in my bonnet I can go back to the time when I had never heard the words acting technique, improvisation or blank verse.

## Early Days, School and University

Even before my début as Moth I can remember that the family atmosphere had a theatrical flavour. My father, grandfather and uncles on both sides were doctors but both my parents were passionately interested in amateur theatre and belonged to the Derby Shakespeare Society. This had been in existence since 1908 and had started several young actors on a theatrical career, notably Alan Bates, who played Prince Arthur in *King John*, Prince Edward in *Richard III* and Romeo's page for the company over a period of about two years. Given our family background, it was inevitable that my sisters and I would be

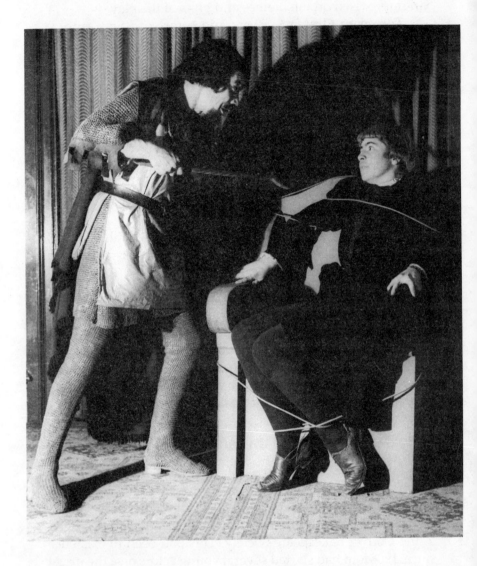

Figure 1: Alan Bates as Arthur in the Derby Shakespeare Society's production of *King John*, March 1949. Courtesy of Mrs M. Bates.

enlisted to play small parts from an early age. Hence my introduction into the theatre as Moth. However, my interest in Shakespeare had been kindled before that.

A typical example of an incident which had fired my imagination as a child occurred during a thunder-storm in Wales. The family was on holiday near Lake Bala. We children were lying asleep in bed in a small hotel when a violent crash of thunder woke us; forked lightning lit up the room. We cowered under the bed-clothes. And then, at the height of the storm, the bedroom door opened and our mother appeared as Lady Macbeth in the sleep-walking scene moaning,

"Yet here's a spot . . . Out, dammed spot!"

We screamed with terror and had to be pacified by our father. When he remonstrated with her she replied, unabashed, "But I was only trying to take their minds off the storm." And, as far as I was concerned, she did. The power of the words and the drama of the occasion haunted my mind for a long time.

Charles Doran's touring company came to the Grand Theatre, Derby from time to time. He brought some of the actors to our house after the performances. We used to hear the talk and laughter floating up the stairs far into the night, but I only recall meeting Charles Doran once, one day at teatime.

The usual school productions fed my enthusiasm for acting. My first words on any stage were

"Brekkek Kek Kek Koax Koax
Koax as we grow in the mire."

The most vivid recollection I have of that performance of *The Frogs of Aristophanes* was crouching with my fellow frogs in the wings of the school stage. Our costumes, of green and yellow sateen, were made so that we could not stand upright in them. I saw the yellow cotton which covered my chest heaving up and down. I could hardly breathe because of the combination of excitement and stage fright. I was convinced that the whole success of Aristophane's play depended on my getting those words right.

Later on in Junior School, we staged *A Kiss for Cinderella*, by J. M. Barrie as an end of term production. I had overcome some of my nerves by this time and enjoyed playing the leading part. My parents appeared to be pleasantly surprised by my efforts and, in fact, for years afterwards, even when I was acting in the West End, my mother would often comment, to my extreme annoyance, "Yes, but you aren't as good in this as you were in *A Kiss for Cinderella*."

Appearances with the Derby Shakespeare Society fed my special interest in Shakespeare, although the chief impression made on me by *The Merry Wives of Windsor* was of the long print dress and cotton kerchief I wore as one of the children who mocked Falstaff in the Windsor Forest scene at the end of the play,

> "Pinch him and burn him and turn him about
> Till candles and starlight and moonshine be out."

At boarding school, Penrhôs College, I was fortunate in having a brilliant, though somewhat eccentric, drama teacher. 'Elocution', as it was called then, was an extra subject and the small number of us who took it were regarded as being somewhat peculiar by the rest of the school. Miss Barber used to embarrass us by marching us around the school grounds doing exercises for voice production. One of her favourites was the one in which we had to pinch our noses while we walked in time to the words intoning,

> She left the web she left the loom
> She made three paces through the room
> She saw the water lily bloom
> She saw the helmet and the plume
> She looked down to Camelot.

You can imagine the derisive amusement this caused as we circled the playing fields where our schoolmates were playing hockey.

When I left school I was set on a stage career and determined to go to a drama school. However, my father, in his wisdom as it afterwards turned out, stipulated that I must get some other qualification first. I asked whether a degree in English Literature would be sufficient? He agreed.

I wanted to go up to Oxford, but as Mathematics and Latin were my two weakest subjects, this was out of the question. However, I shall always be grateful that I went to Birmingham University because at that time the English Department was one of the best in the country. I had as tutors Helen Gardner, then at the beginning of her distinguished career, and Professor A. M. D. Hughes, the authority on Shelley and, as lecturers, Professor Ernest de Selincourt and Louis McNeice, whose thankless task it was,to coach the first year Honours undergraduates in Latin. I thought he had an aloof, Spanish look but admired him from afar. I was shattered during one of his lectures when he fixed me with a stern eye and said "If Miss Laurie would pay less attention to her crib and more to Vergil's text, she might get on better." Latin was always a struggle.

Professor Hughes was small, frail and saintly-looking. It was startling when he walked to the front of the big lecture-room and began his lecture on *Hamlet* with the words "Now I could drink blood", uttered quietly but with an astonishing, intense ferocity. R. D. Smith, who later became a brilliant Radio Producer at the BBC, had also been tutored by him and used to say "When Professor Hughes asks one to open the window one goes like a knight in search of the Holy Grail."

In my first year at University, Reggie Smith and Dorothy Reynolds were the leading figures in the Dramatic Society. Dorothy went on to play leading parts in the West End and was co-author of the musical *Salad Days*.

Of course, every minute I could spare was devoted to acting and directing. When the actor playing the part of Hero, in my production of *Much Ado About Nothing,* fell ill I took over the part. My mother came over to see it. She sent a note round in the interval - "You've too much rouge on and your ears are showing." This, though undoubtedly true, did nothing to build up my confidence in the second half of the show. I found John Barber, later the drama critic for *The Daily Telegraph*, more helpful. He took a keen interest in all our efforts.

During an undergraduate review at the Prince of Wales Theatre, Birmingham, I had my first, and only, experience of being pelted with eggs and booed. I was playing in a sketch opposite Henry Reed (who was to write arguably the best poem to come out of the Second World War - *The Naming of Parts*) and we both shrugged off the episode with, what I think now, was surprising equanimity.

During the vacations I played two more parts with the Derby Shakespeare Society - Prince Edward in *Richard III* and Titania in *A Midsummer Night's Dream*. I thoroughly enjoyed being one of the Princes in the Tower but this performance marked the end of my youthful confidence on the stage. I may have done well as Prince Edward; not so as Titania. The reasons for this were three-fold: I had to wear an unbecoming wig; I was given two lots of direction - at rehearsals and at home; and I was looking back over my shoulder at University and my social life there. I have always thought, moreover, that Titania is a particularly difficult part to play.

## Royal Academy of Dramatic Art

When I came down from Birmingham I auditioned for the Royal Academy of Dramatic Art (RADA) and was accepted. I must say that it was easier to get a place there in those days than it is now, when the numbers applying are so much greater.

I think the fact that I was slightly older than the average student at RADA at that time was an advantage. Even so, in my first term I was on a see-saw between agonising anxiety and near rapture. I found that it was one thing to rehearse a scene in my digs (to my own satisfaction) but quite another to perform it in front of my peers in class. I would stammer, forget the lines, go crimson in the face with embarrassment and end up near to tears.

Liz Pisk taught us movement. We were hypnotised by her vitality and enthusiasm. During one of our early lessons on period movement she suddenly pulled her practice skirt up between her legs and tucked the hem in at her waist. "Now I em a MEN" she announced to the surprised class. Years later when I was out in Hong Kong adjudicating at the Speech and Drama Festival I met a member of that class, Austin Coates. "Can you still do a stage fall?" I asked him. "Yes, of course. Can you?" Thereupon we both collapsed on to the floor to the astonishment of his Chinese friends.

I enjoyed my time at RADA in spite of the fact that I was being given so much conflicting advice from the tutors there: you should play in Shakespeare; you should concentrate on comedy. The most devastating counsel came from Henry Cass: "Don't go into the theatre, go home, marry and have lots of beautiful babies." I was in such a state of turmoil one day, that I collapsed in tears on a bench in Regent's Park. I was comforted by a final year student who said,

"All your tutors can teach you something. Learn to take from each one only what you feel is going to be useful to you."

This was helpful, sound advice and I have passed it on since to many students.

Whilst I was studying at RADA, a modern dress version of *Julius Caesar* was performed at the Embassy Theatre, Swiss Cottage (now the home of the Central School) and later transferred to what was then His Majesty's Theatre. Henry Cass was the director and Godfrey Tearle played Brutus, Eric Portman - Mark Antony and Clifford Evans - Cassius. It was updated to the period of the Second World War, the period of the dictatorships of Hitler and Mussolini. Several RADA students were chosen to be in the crowd. I was immensely proud to be given one line "Noble Antony, go up", which was the cue for Eric Portman to mount the rostrum. Some of us were supposed to be housewives out shopping. We wore headscarves and carried shopping bags. Every night when the crowd scenes were over, I shot round to the gallery to watch the rest of the play. Godfrey Tearle and Clifford Evans were electric in the quarrel scene and Eric Portman compelling in his "Friends, Romans, Countrymen" speech. I was amused to see how, in the modern battle scenes, Tearle would gather his army greatcoat around him as if it were a toga.

On leaving RADA I could not, at first, get a job in the theatre. However, I was asked to organise the first Drama Department at the Arts Educational School which, up till then, had concentrated mainly on ballet. This was a challenge as the gifted youngsters there were wonderfully expressive in movement but, at first, totally inexpressive in speech. John Gilpin stood out from the rest and was obviously destined for a brilliant career. Also at the school was a promising student called Jill Pyrke. She and I appeared in Leicester Repertory's production of *Dear Octopus*. She afterwards changed her name to Gillian Lynne and is the world-famous choreographer of *Cats* and many other productions.

## Repertory

After a year at the Arts Educational School I managed, through *Spotlight*, to get a job in weekly repertory at Farnham in the old Castle Theatre. The first few weeks there were nightmarish since the other actors seemed to be working at twice the speed that I was. My cues came up at me with bewildering rapidity. The rest of the company seemed able to learn their lines effortlessly and to cope with complicated stage business whilst saying them. I could not even pour cups of tea and time my lines whilst doing it without holding up rehearsals, to the ill-concealed impatience of the cast and the weary resignation of the director. I felt like Alice in *Through the Looking Glass*,

"And still the Queen kept crying faster! Faster! But Alice felt she could not go faster."

Gradually, however, I learned to relax and handling props actually became a pleasure. Remembering those early days in repertory makes me sympathetic towards those students who find lighting a cigarette confidently on cue a difficult operation.

I found that movement, in general, was difficult. During the first three years in the theatre I felt that I was stiff and awkward. When I became depressed about this I reminded myself of John Gielgud's confession,

12

"Until I realised that I was handicapped by a strange way of standing and a still stranger way of walking, I really thought acting might be a comparatively simple matter."

I stayed at Farnham for eight months playing a variety of parts from Elsie, the adenoidal child, in Coward's *Fumed Oak* to Madame Heist in Strindberg's *Easter*. This, of course, was invaluable experience. But weekly repertory was gruelling. We had no days off as Sundays were spent in learning lines and assembling our costumes for the following week's play. We dress-rehearsed on Mondays and opened with the new play on Monday nights. Tuesday mornings found us rehearsing Act I of the following week's play. We usually had two run-throughs of the play before the dress rehearsal. One either sank or swam.

When I was graciously given a week off after playing a succession of juvenile leads, I found that I was required to sit behind the stage on a high stool. I was draped in a black cloak and had to move the minute hand of the clock during the performances of *Ten Minute Alibi*. One night, because of a misunderstanding between the actor playing the murderer and myself and the resulting struggle over which way to move the minute hand, the mystified audience saw a performance of 'Twenty Minute Alibi'! As I had shown a certain reluctance about being employed in this way during my so-called 'week-off', the management said, "Oh, but we're putting you in the programme - as Miss Tick-Tock."

I was sometimes cast in middle-aged and elderly parts. I regarded anything over fifty as being very old indeed and creaked around the stage like a ninety-year old. When I was playing the old lady in *Easter*, I caused the rest of the company to 'corpse' (dry up with helpless laughter) on one occasion. It was our custom during performances to study next week's play in the wings. There was an old-fashioned, round, iron stove there and I was standing by it some yards from the entrance to the stage, studying my part for the following week, when suddenly I heard my cue. The actors on stage heard the slap of the script going down on top of the stove, wildly scampering feet and then the door opened and the oldest woman in creation

Figure 2: A photograph of Rona Laurie at the beginning of her stage career by Angus McBean.

tottered on to the centre of the stage. No one could speak. I was indignant and quite unaware of what had upset them.

Remembering lines is obviously one of the worst problems of weekly repertory. First nights were to be dreaded, to be got through as best we could. This created a marvellous sense of camaraderie in the company. We learned to get ourselves out of trouble - had to, in fact, as the stage manager could not always be relied on to give a helpful prompt - or even to be 'on the book.'

During one particular first night our resources were tried to the utmost. It was a play by an unknown author and we had a new assistant stage manager who had been sent down from London to replace an a.s.m. who had not been able to stand the strain any longer. The recruit was enthusiastic but raw. We were, for some reason, playing in curtains: came the last act, the dénouement of the play, and a monumental 'dry' from our leading man. "Prompt," he muttered - silence from the wings. He improvised a bit and then came back to the sticking-point. "*Prompt*," he hissed. From behind the curtains came the whispered words "Whose line?" "*Any* bloody line," he shouted and tore the curtains aside to reveal the assistant stage manager almost crying with anxiety. He snatched the book from her and found the place. The words he needed were "Who's lying under that stone?" We continued with as much gravity as we could muster.

All this will probably seem very strange to today's actors who often have the luxury of three to six week's rehearsal in repertory. But, provided one did not stay in repertory too long, it was a good training-ground.

Nowadays, drama schools proliferate and are regarded by would-be actors as the main way into the theatre. Some of our most successful, older actors, however, have never been to drama school. They have entered the profession by another door - through provincial repertory companies. They started their apprenticeship as humble tea-makers, sweepers of the stage and general dogs-bodies to the company. But they were there every night learning their craft, by watching, by understudying, by playing small parts. If they were lucky, they graduated to playing leading parts in the company. They were cast in suitable and unsuitable roles; they were under fire at an early age. As long as they did not acquire stage tricks and a superficial approach it was valuable experience.

There is much to be said for both forms of entry into the acting profession. But, in losing so many good repertory companies the theatre has also lost useful nurseries of talent.

## Touring

I have a great regard for the benefits to be gained by touring, if the actor approaches it as a means of enriching his experience by handling different kinds of audiences and different sized stages. Such experience was certainly to be gained by anyone who joined The English Classical Players. After I had been in repertory for eight months, this company gave me my first taste of touring.

We were a curious mix of raw young actors and elderly men. We travelled the length and breadth of England in an old bus, driven by the company handyman with great dash and nervous energy. Our wardrobe swayed from hangers at the back of the bus.

We had a repertoire of three plays: *As You Like It*, *The Tempest* and Shaw's *You Never Can Tell*. We played out of doors, whatever the weather, in the grounds of schools. The scenery was minimal, which was just as well, because we had to unload it, set it up and strike it after the show and then reload it. It was not unusual for us to play a matinée of *As You Like It* and then drive fifty miles to give an evening performance of *You Never Can Tell*.

Sometimes we had very little time to inspect the site where we were going to perform and to decide where we were going to make our exits and entrances. This led to an awkward moment in *As You Like It*, when Rosalind, having been banished by the Duke, her uncle, was fleeing the court with Celia and Touchstone. Rosalind was walking down a narrow path, only to be confronted by the Duke and his Courtiers approaching on the same path. It was too late to turn back. As banisher and banished squeezed past each other heads were averted and each pretended not to see the other. I can't remember the audience laughing at this; I expect that they were too bewildered by this unexpected twist in the plot.

Alfred Burke was a romantic Orlando and Richard O'Donoghue (later Administrator at RADA) was Oliver. I enjoyed playing Celia and found *As You Like It* much less taxing than *The Tempest* in which I was doubling the parts of 'Trinculo - a drunken jester' with 'Iris, Goddess of the Rainbow.' This was due to the shortage of men. I had to under-dress and during the quick change at the end of the play the cast used to gather in the wings to watch me tearing off my parti-coloured jester's costume to reveal the crumpled chiffon and classical hairstyle of the goddess before I emerged in the Masque,

"the Queen o' th' sky,
Whose wat'ry arch and messenger am I."

Once, in winter we were stranded penniless in the wilds and had to spend the night in the bus. One resourceful member of the company seized one of the costumes from the back to act as a blanket. We all followed suit, those getting hold of the noblemen's heavy robes doing best. I was sorry for the person who had to make do with Iris's costume.

This tour was a period of great enjoyment. We were a lively group who got on pretty well together, despite the inevitable emotional entanglements. When the tour finished, I returned to Farnham, after having found myself a London agent. Out of the blue a postcard arrived telling me of an audition Ralph Lynn was holding for a revival of *Thark*, one of the plays from the famous Ben Travers/Ralph Lynn/Tom Walls season at the Aldwych. I had never played in farce, but I travelled hopefully up to London. It was my first big audition and I was amazed at the number of young actresses queuing up to read. Most of them looked sophisticated and seemed to be experienced. I was conscious that I was neither. Just before my turn came to go up on the stage, someone told me that the part of Winifred Shotter, for which I was reading, had been almost definitely cast. Undaunted, I went on and started to read.

Funnily enough, I didn't feel nervous. After a few minutes I was called down into the stalls and offered the part. My heart was beating so hard that I could hardly breathe, let alone speak. I telephoned my somewhat surprised agent and was told that I could collect the contract that afternoon. This, of course, was a break, a wonderful opportunity at that point in my career. It was the beginning of a long apprenticeship learning the art of farce from a master -Ralph Lynn, whom Ben Travers described as the greatest farce actor that he had ever known.

I was now engaged for a series of tours of revivals of the Aldwych farces of the 1920's and 1930's. We began with *Thark* and *Tons of Money*. Later I played in *Rookery Nook* and we came to London in a new farce which Ben Travers wrote for Ralph Lynn and Robertson Hare, *Outrageous Fortune*. This was produced at the Winter Garden Theatre, Drury Lane, now rebuilt as the New London.

## The West End

I had been working solidly for eleven years in the theatre, learning my job, before I came to the West End. In the four years that followed *Outrageous Fortune*, I was playing various juvenile parts and had a long period as an understudy at the Savoy Theatre during the run of *The Last of Mrs Cheyney*. Once again I was able to watch fine actors night after night. This cast, headed by Jack Buchanan and Coral Browne, was star-studded. Athene Seyler's performance was an object lesson in the art of playing comedy.

One night, the girl I was understudying arrived so late in the theatre that I was told to go on. I had a short scene with Jack Buchanan. With typical generosity he played it with his back to the audience, giving me the stage. It was at that moment, looking out at the auditorium and seeing the glimmer of faces, row on row, that I had a sudden flashback to that similar moment, years before when I was lying on the stage of the Temperance Hall, Derby as Moth. Again I had a sensation of rightness.

But by now, I felt, my days as a juvenile were numbered. I did not want to make a record as being the oldest one in the business. But what now? I had worked for H. M. Tennant and for Firth Shephard; had toured extensively; and played in the West End. However, I was not a 'name'. I was old enough to play 'Mother' parts, but didn't look it. I decided I would fill in the time with work associated with the theatre until I was ready to come back to audition for older parts.

## The Guildhall School of Music and Drama

It was at this point that a position became vacant at the Guildhall School of Music and Drama, then in John Carpenter Street, off the Embankment. The School was looking for someone with professional stage experience and a degree, to lecture on English Literature to the drama students. I was interviewed for the job and got it. I had no idea at the time that this would involve me in more than just a few hours a week. It was, however, a change of direction. I was asked to do more and more work lecturing, taking classes for student actors and teachers and giving individual coaching. I became Head of the Department of Drama in Education and subsequently ran the postgraduate course in Elizabethan and Jacobean Theatre.

The atmosphere in the Guildhall School in that Victorian building near the Thames was warm and friendly. I particularly enjoyed teatime in the professor's club. One would sit at the long table listening to famous singers talking 'shop' - Parry Jones, Norman Walker, Dennis Noble, Joseph Hislop. I became fascinated with vocal technique as it affected both the singing and the speaking voice. Of course, I had withdrawal symptoms from acting and, in fact, still have. However I found, and still find, it rewarding to pass on the knowledge gained in the theatre to young drama students and, more recently, to the students at the Opera School of the Royal College of Music.

This chapter has dealt with my personal involvement with the theatre. Now let us move on to specific areas of the actor's art and craft.

# Chapter Two

# Voice and Speech

"Speak the speech I pray you . . . trippingly on the tongue . . ."
*Hamlet*

## Voice Production

When Tommaso Salvini, the great Italian actor, was asked what qualities one must have to play tragedy, he replied "Voice, voice and more voice." This statement is worth exploring since, although we have some fine-voiced actors today, it is in their vocal technique that the majority are weakest. Audiences are complaining more and more frequently that they cannot hear what is being said on the stage. And yet new methods of voice production and systems of exercises are constantly being advocated. The trouble is that much of this theory is not related sufficiently to the practical work. The proof of the pudding is in the eating. Whether a method of voice production is successful or not can only be judged by results, by what the audience hears during an actual performance. Too often, however they do not hear the actor, or even if he is audible he is not distinct.

The actor's voice is a vitally important tool of his trade. How can he ensure that he is always heard and understood in all parts of the theatre, whatever the size of the auditorium? Let us begin with basics. It is surprising how many people cannot define the difference between *voice*, *speech* and *modulation*. In layman's language the terms are used indiscriminately.

*Voice* may be described as the raw material - the sound that issues from the mouth. You could hear the sound of someone's voice in the next room and could register the fact that it is deep or high-pitched, although you could not necessarily distinguish the words, could not understand what was being said. *Speech* is the shaping of the sound into vowels, consonants and words, that is, it involves enunciation, articulation and pronunciation. *Modulation* is the expressive use of voice and speech.

To use an analogy: imagine a man going into a tailor's shop to choose the material for a suit. It may be good quality material or shoddy. That is the equivalent of *voice*. Next, the material has to be cut and made up. That process may be compared to *speech*. Finally, the way the man wears the suit may be compared with *modulation*. That is the expressive use, the style of his voice and speech.

There are basic elements involved in all three processes. Unless the actor understands these, he is likely to have problems with his voice at some point in his career. These elements should be explored in a logical order and with common sense. The ultimate question to answer concerning any method of voice production is - does it work? Some actors try to follow an abstract approach, only to find during a performance that their voice production is not able to cope with the demands made upon it.

So, first things first. It is essential to be able to relax both physically and mentally. This means freeing the body and mind

21

from undue tension. Relaxation exercises are often concentrated only on the body. They are more effective if they are linked to an imaginative idea or a series of ideas linked to a theme.

To take a simple example: imagine that you are lying on an exposed mountain-top, flat on your back. Night comes on and the temperature starts to drop. You become colder and colder and begin to freeze from the toes upwards. You tense your toes, feet, ankles, calves, thighs, stomach, torso, shoulders, arms, wrists, hands, neck and face. You are tense from your toes to the top of your head. It is quite difficult, at first, to isolate the various parts of the body, one after the other, without anticipating the next stage of the exercise. But this ability comes with practice. Hold this tensed position for thirty seconds and then imagine that the night has passed, the sun has come out and is starting to thaw you out from the top of your head down to your toes. Now the process is reversed. You relax the muscles of your face, neck, shoulders, arms, wrists, hands, torso, stomach, thighs, calves, ankles, feet and toes. Now imagine that you are thoroughly thawed out and warm from top to toe. Then allow your thoughts to drift. Five minutes in a relaxed state like this, preferably in a darkened studio or room, are enormously helpful in relieving an actor of stress.

Two important points emerge from this exercise: the value of linking bodily and mental relaxation; and the value of alternating the tension and relaxation of the muscles. Mental relaxation is generally more difficult to achieve than physical.

A further aid to relaxation is laughter. This may be genuine and unforced or it may start as a technical exercise and develop into the real thing. We know that life is real, that life is earnest in the precarious profession of the theatre, but a sense of humour is a priceless quality for it brings with it, as well as the ability to relax, a sense of proportion. An exercise for general relaxation along the lines that I have described may be used after more specific exercises, concentrating on different areas where tension first builds up. This varies from person to person. It may be in the back of the neck, the throat, the face or shoulders: some people unconsciously tense their hands. Exercises to free the neck and throat muscles, the shoulders and torso are particularly helpful.

Think of your head as being very heavy - a ball of lead. Let it drop forward, then rotate it slowly from left to right, trying to get the ear down to your shoulder, *not* the shoulder up to the ear. Lift your head slightly as you reach the back to avoid pinching the nerves of the neck. Then repeat the exercise from right to left. Be careful not to overdo this at first, as it can cause giddiness.

Edward Heath, the former Prime Minister, has unwittingly provided a good exercise for the shoulders by the way he laughs. Mime laughter, lifting your shoulders rapidly up and down. Ballet dancers, who often have great difficulty in freeing their shoulders when projecting the voice, find this exercise and the following one particularly helpful.

Stand sideways to the wall and imagine that the point of your elbow is covered in chalk and that the wall is a blackboard. Raise your elbow and let the forearm hang down so that there is a straight line from the shoulder to the point of the elbow. Slowly rotate your elbow in a forward direction describing an imaginary circle on the blackboard. Do this three times and then rotate your elbow three times in a backward direction. Repeat the exercise with the other elbow. Stand clear of the wall and do the exercise with both elbows at once, gradually increasing the pace to a swinging rhythm. Imagine a ball and socket with the top of the arm moving in the shoulder socket. Remember to keep your head erect and not to poke it forward.

A former colleague of mine, John Holgate, had a favourite exercise which he called *Cursing the Unkind Gods*. One should imagine a hostile presence in the skies, then tense your entire body, raise your arms, clench your fists and shake them vigorously and with feeling. Make aggressive sounds. Then imagine that you are struck by a bolt from the heavens and slowly collapse into a drooping position. This exercise is therapeutic and usually enjoyed. One can let off steam and get rid of feelings of hostility.

Suppose that our imaginary actor is now able to achieve both mental and physical relaxation. The next thing to consider is posture. It is astonishing how often this essential part of an actor's training is either forgotten or not given enough consideration. We live at a time when household furniture encourages slouched positions. I am thinking particularly of the bean-bag style seat, of heaped cushions on the floor, of soft padded chairs and sofas.

One notices poor posture most when watching Restoration and late Eighteenth Century plays. Very few actors can wear the costume with the correct period deportment. The men are more guilty than the women in this respect. The Restoration Courtier may look splendidly in period from the front, wearing a historically accurate, magnificently designed costume. It is only when he presents his side or back view to the audience that the illusion is lost, because of his slovenly way of standing. Uniforms of any kind, of any period, also demand upright deportment and an erect carriage of the head.

The way a person stands affects his voice-production. Obviously, upright posture is unsuitable for many characters and for many parts in plays, particularly today, but if the actor has practised voice production exercises using the correct posture he should be able to produce his voice properly, regardless of his position on stage. Kenneth Branagh had a problem of this kind in *Henry V* when he had to deliver the "Once more into the breach, dear friends, once more" speech clinging precariously to the side of the walls of Harfleur, but he managed to solve it.

Why is it so important to practise to achieve good posture? Let us consider what happens when the posture is habitually poor. It is the breathing apparatus that is affected most adversely. When the shoulders are bent it is difficult to expand the lungs sufficiently and so the intake of breath is reduced.

Of the many exercises for good posture, I have found this one to be the most useful. Stand with your feet together, about six inches from the wall, let your buttocks touch the wall and then bend over your feet, with straight knees. Gradually unroll, feeling the vertebrae of the spine pressing, one by one, against the wall. Then inch backwards until your heels touch the wall. Your back will now hollow slightly. Be sure that your shoulders

24

are not hunched as your back moves up and that your chin is level. Then walk forward and relax slightly. One word of warning: do not try this exercise on a slippery floor or in slippery, soled shoes.

A simpler exercise is to imagine that you are a puppet and that someone is holding a string, which is attached to the top of your spine, and is pulling it upwards. I do not despise the old Rank Charm School exercise of walking about the room with a book balanced on the head. This is particularly effective in ensuring that the chin is held level. If it is held too high or too low the book falls off. If the chin is held too high the muscles of the throat will be stretched, putting a strain on the voice and, if too low, they will be constricted. In both cases voice production will suffer.

Pages and pages have been written on the subject of breathing and breath control and how they affect voice production. Conflicting advice has been given and there is some confusion in the use of technical terms such as 'inter-costal diaphragmatic', 'rib-reserve' and 'whole-chest breathing.' I have seen drama students and actors struggling to breathe 'correctly' and becoming tense and worried in the process.

Over the years, I have modified my ideas on this vexed subject, particularly on the best method of controlling the outgoing air. I no longer think that hard and fast rules should be applied, but that the student and actor should be encouraged to find out and use whichever method works for him. However, there is no doubt in my mind that he should use the inter-costal diaphragmatic method for inhalation as this ensures the maximum intake of air.

Here is a simple exercise which, if practised diligently, will ensure an adequate supply of breath. Expel the breath from your lungs on an 'S' sound to a mental count of twenty. Imagine that your lungs are balloons with a pin-prick in each so that the air is escaping gradually. Then lift your rib-cage up and out. This rib-swing will cause the air to be drawn through your open mouth to fill the vacuum in your lungs. Think of a pair of bellows. On exhalation the sides are dropping, but when the sides are lifted in inhalation, the air rushes in through the spout of the bellows - your mouth. When the ribs swing up and out, the sides of the diaphragm (large muscle separating the thorax from the abdomen) are lifted and its central tendon drops about an inch and a quarter, allowing for expansion at the base of the lungs. The lifting of the rib-cage gives lateral, frontal and dorsal expansion.

The ribs are lifted by means of muscles which lie between them - the external inter-costals. The strength of these muscles varies in people from being almost negligible to very powerful. But gradually, through exercise, these muscles can be strengthened and brought into full use.

Now that the lungs are filled with air the process of exhalation starts. It is at this stage that there are two main schools of thought. The earlier one insists that the rib-cage is held out during exhalation until the breath is nearly exhausted and then the rib-cage is allowed to drop, the latter one allows the rib-cage to drop gradually as the breath is exhaled. Advocates of the first method believe that this gives greater control. I now teach the second, later method because I find that some actors, particularly women, find it difficult and inhibiting to hold the rib-cage out during a performance.

Whichever method is used, the out-going breath should be controlled by the abdominal press. This technical expression is often misunderstood and sometimes mispronounced: I have heard it referred to as the 'abominable' press! It describes an action which is, in very simplified terms, the contraction of the transverse abdominal muscle which is linked to muscles which control the return of the diaphragm to its former position arching into the thorax. This exerts gradual pressure on the base of the lungs and the breath is exhaled in a steady stream.

Once the student is able to use rib-swing to fill his lungs, he can start exhalation exercises. He should count aloud from one to ten on a fairly low-pitched, full tone and gradually increase the number he can speak on one breath. He should eventually be able to speak at least three lines of blank verse without strain and without exhausting his breath reserves. Some actors employ a third method of exhalation whereby they keep the rib-cage out all the time and renew the breath by means of the diaphragm. This method is used frequently during highly-charged, emotional speeches. Once a performer realises that he has the vocal power and the ability (which comes from good breath control) to sustain the voice over long phrases, he seldom goes back to former habits of shallow, uncontrolled breathing.

Working with opera students as well as with actors has reinforced my conviction of the value of studying phrasing in relation to breathing. I encourage them to work out and then mark in their scripts exactly where they are going to take a breath. In other words, to apply the same discipline to their speaking voice as they would to their singing voice. Once this technique has been mastered it can be forgotten and the mind can concentrate on the meaning and feeling behind the words.

We will assume that our imaginary actor is now free from undue tension, has good posture and is able to control his inhalation and exhalation. The next step is to achieve a forward placing of the voice on the lips. The sound should pass through an open throat, be directed onto the hard palate, which acts as a sounding board, and then be borne on the lips. Most good actors have voices which are placed forward. Alec Guinness is an outstanding example. His voice is projected without apparent effort and, even when speaking very quietly, has enormous resonance - as have the voices of Kenneth Branagh, Michael Gambon, Nigel Hawthorne, Derek Jacobi and Robert Lindsay. The forward-placed voices of Judi Dench and Dorothy Tutin have an appealing, distinctive quality.

Practising the following exercises will help forward plac-ing. Firstly, it is essential that the muscles of the throat are not constricted, so the head-rolling exercises already mentioned should be used to free the neck and throat. Next, the soft palate should be exercised to ensure that the opening from the throat to the back of the mouth is free and that the movement of the soft palate is flexible. Some performers and public speakers have a lazy soft palate and do not raise it sufficiently after 'K', 'G' and

'NG' sounds. The exercise is a repetition of these three sounds interspersed with an 'AH' sound - thus 'K AH G AH UNG AH'.

Finally ,the actor should say 'M' and hum it. It is important that he feels a vibration on the lips whilst he is doing this. It is possible to make a humming sound without using them, therefore he should test that the sound is borne on the lips by gently plucking his lower lip with his finger, whilst continuing to hum. When the sound is interrupted he will know that his placing is right. Most people can do this without too much difficulty.

The next question to be considered is how to ensure that the resonance in the voice is balanced. Resonance is the ringing quality which is caused by the vibration of air in the resonance cavities. The most important of these are the pharynx, situated just above the vocal cords, the nasal cavities and the mouth, which is the biggest. Balanced resonance implies a sound in which no single resonator is over working or dominating the others.

One hears examples of unbalanced resonance every day of the week. There is the deep, husky, pharyngeal tone artificially produced by some actresses ("Dah-ling") not, it must be said, without this characteristic sometimes becoming a commercial asset. This artificiality has nothing to do with a natural, slightly husky voice which can be most attractive. Think of the voices of Dorothy Tutin and Judi Dench. Then there is the 'plummy' tone produced by too much mouth resonance. This sound, unfortunately, is often associated with clergymen and politicians and can suggest pomposity.

Probably the most common example of unbalanced resonance is found amongst public speakers, broadcasters and speakers on television. This is caused by too much nasal resonance. In extreme cases it sounds as if the speaker is suffering from a heavy head cold, or has blocked sinuses (he may indeed have blocked sinuses).

In the unlikely event of my being cast on the late Roy Plumley's desert island with one student and being only allowed to take one voice exercise with me, it would be the resonator scale. This is the repetition of a sequence of vowel sounds which ensure that the main resonating cavities are used.

There is a well-known mnemonic to remind one of the sequence: 'who would know aught of art must learn and then take his ease'. This is sometimes rendered 'as who would know aught of art must learn and then shape fit speech'. I prefer the latter variation, since one can never afford to slacken off in voice and speech work. If the vowel sounds are taken out of the sentence thus:

(would)

OO (who) U (neutral vowel) OH (know) AW (aught)

O (of) AH (art) U (must) ER (learn) A (and)

E (then) AY (shape) I (fit) EE (speech)

and an 'M' sound is put in front of them:

MOO MU (neutral) MOH MAW MO MAH MU MER

MA MEH MAY MI MEE

not only will the speaker develop balanced resonance but also forward placing of the voice.

Later on, the exercise can be extended, putting an 'M' sound at the end of the vowel as well as at the beginning:

MOOM MUM (neutral) MOHM MAWM MOM MAHM

MUM MERM MAM MEHM MAYM MIM MEEM

Then 'N' can be substituted for the 'M' sounds:

NOO NU (neutral) NOH NAW NOH NAH etc.

(NB: the sign '—' represents a long vowel and '˘' a short one.)

Our imaginary actor has now gained a well-produced voice by means of the basic elements of relaxation, good posture, efficient breathing and breath control. He has the ability to place the voice forward and to achieve a balanced resonance.

All these elements add up to good tone quality but this, in itself, does not necessarily make a good actor. Tyrone Guthrie once said "Heaven preserve me from actors with good voices." The implication of this remark will be considered in the next chapter on *Modulation*. However, let us first turn to *Speech* - the shaping of sound into vowels, consonants and words.

## Speech

"Is not speech a glory?" asked Thomas Traherne, the seventeenth century mystic. The beauty of spoken English lies in the musical quality of the vowel sounds, which makes it a good language in which to speak verse and play love-scenes, and the firm, astringent quality of the consonants which is useful when an actor has to use satire and invective or to convey precise information.

I am afraid that the following lines from Edward Fitzgerald's translation of the *Rubáiyát* of Omar Khayyam,

"Listen again. One evening at the Close
Of Ramadan ere the better moon arose,
In that old Potter's Shop I stood alone
With the clay Population round in Rows.
And, strange to tell, among that Earthen Lot
Some could articulate, while others not."

came irreverently into my mind the other day, but I forbore from saying them aloud. I do not think that my class of first-year drama students would have appreciated the allusions to "the clay population" or "that Earthen Lot". But the quotation was certainly apt as regards their powers of articulation.

Poets and playwrights have taken advantage of the contrasted qualities of sounds as between vowels and consonants and between the different consonants. Sometimes they do this very obviously as in these well known lines from Alfred Lord Tennyson's *Idylls of the King*:

> "He, stepping down by zigzag paths,
> And juts of pointed rock,
> Came on the shining levels of the lake."

Here the sharp, explosive sounds of 'J', 'P', 'D' and 'T' are contrasted with the liquid 'L' sounds and the long vowels in "came", "shining" and "lake".

Wilfred Owen is versatile in his use of vowels and consonants. Contrast the line "Only the stuttering rifles' rapid rattle" from *Anthem for Doomed Youth*, with the magical use of half-rhymes in *Futility*:

> "Was it for this the clay grew tall?
> 0 what made, fatuous sunbeams toil
> To break earth's sleep at all?"

If the articulation is weak, the power of the consonant is wasted. I am not, of course, advocating a pedantic over-forceful use of consonants. We have all heard speakers over-articulating to such an extent that they get a rebound on final 'D', 'T' and 'K' sounds, for example 'HEAD-ER', 'EIGHT-ER', 'NECK-ER'.

Alec McCowen is a fine example of an actor who can deliver lines at great speed without sacrificing distinctness. On the other hand, I was sitting in the stalls the other day and found that an actress' words were difficult to understand because of her failure to speak the beginnings and ends of the words firmly. The lines drifted with vague musicality.

If the vowels are distorted the subtlety of the language is reduced. This insidious erosion is happening all the time. We frequently hear 'PAH' for 'POWER' and 'AHLAND' for 'IRELAND', for instance.

It is important for an actor who wishes to play a range of parts, including classical ones, to have, in addition to any regional accent he may speak, a pure enunciation of vowel sounds. This, I believe, is an unfashionable point of view today. But imagine the effect on a production of *King Lear* in which the King spoke with Received Pronunciation and Goneril, Regan and Cordelia spoke with Somerset, Midland and Liverpool accents respectively. One would suspect that the old man had owned at least a bicycle!

It is a symptom of the rather cavalier approach to speech that one seldom hears convincing and consistent accents throughout a cast in a play in which the actors are required to speak in some accent other than their own. This applies particularly to American, Irish and North Country dialogue. Inconsistencies in accent are always noticed and commented on by audiences. An actor to whom I mentioned this said, "Oh, you're either good at accents or you're not." Admittedly, but the ear can be trained to pick up and reproduce sounds and speech 'tunes'. The ability to reproduce different accents should surely be part of an actor's equipment and an important part of his training at drama school. Mike Yarwood's brilliance in vocal impersonation came not only from his keen ear but from prodigious hard work.

Acting is an art of communication and the actor is only effective in so far as he is able to get across what he is saying to an audience. Articulation is a key factor and the organs involved are the tongue, teeth, lips, gums and the hard and soft palates.

An exercise has already been given to make the soft palate more flexible. Much can be done through exercises, to strengthen the tongue-tip, particularly in its formation of 'S', 'T', 'D', 'N', 'L' and 'R' sounds. There are many in the profession with actual speech faults such as an over-sibilant 'S' sound or a weak 'R' sound. One of the reasons for the prevalence of the over-sibilant 'S' sound amongst actors is that children who have difficulty with 'S' are often encouraged to take speech-training lessons and many of them, in this way, acquire a love of acting from an early age.

How can one strengthen the tongue-tip? There are numerous recommended exercises. I find that the rapid alternation of 'T' and 'D' sounds is useful:

TTTTTTDDDDDDTTTTTTDDDDDDTTTTTT

Assuming that there is no difficulty in making these sounds, a Gilbert and Sullivan patter song can be used, like this one from *Ruddigore* - "I shall go at once to Roderic and make him an oration." Every verse ends with a repetition of the word 'matter' - "So

32

it really doesn't matter, matter, matter, matter, matter etc." However, tongue-twisters generally should be used with discretion and only when the consonants can be made accurately. If, for example, someone who has difficulty with 'R' sounds and substitutes a 'W' practises saying, "around the rugged rocks the ragged rascals ran" he will only be rehearsing the fault - "Awound the wugged wocks the wagged wascals wan."

Faulty 'S' sounds may arise from a variety of causes. It may be through wrong positioning of the tongue-tip. This should be placed on the teeth-ridge behind the upper front teeth. The air is then forced down a narrow channel in the centre of the tongue.

Or it may be caused by a gap in the upper front teeth. If this is the case the lower position can be tried. That is the tongue tip is placed behind the lower front teeth and the blade arched up. A minority of people make their 'S' sounds in this way. This method can also be tried if the speaker experiences difficulty in placing the tongue-tip correctly behind the upper front teeth.

It is helpful to approach the sound through a 'T'. 'Tsetse' is an useful word, as in tsetse fly, and can be practised in order to encourage the tongue tip into the right position. Many people cannot make this sound at first and pronounce it without the first 'T'. However, with practice the tongue can be persuaded to make the shift in position from the 'T' to the 'S'.

A weak 'R' sound is sometimes deliberately adopted by a speaker (not generally by an actor) in the belief that it adds refinement to speech, for example, 've'y' for 'very'. This speech habit is not an advantage for an actor unless he is using it in a calculated characterisation for a 'Hooray Henry' or a 'Chinless Wonder' part. If it is a genuine fault, a good way of correcting it is first by strengthening the tongue tip and then by practising a string of words beginning with 'R' prefaced by 'ER':

ER-RABBIT, ER-REBEL, ER-RIDER,

ER-ROSE, ER-RUDDER, ER-RING.

The tongue is encouraged to curl back on the 'ER' sound before flicking forward on the 'R'.

33

Or the 'R' can be approached through a 'D' sound. The sequences -

MIDDER MIDDER MIDDER MIDDER MIRROR

and,

VEDDY VEDDY VEDDY VEDDY VERY

can be repeated. When a 'W' is substituted for a 'R' sound, 'Wose' for 'Rose', the position required for the 'R' has to be practised, that is, the position of the tongue-tip when it flicks past the hard palate.

Careless articulation sometimes produces an unfortunate combination of sounds. Instead of 'A flea in her ear', you get 'A flea in her **Rear**' or 'Go shake your **Rears**' instead of 'Go shake your ears'. One should guard against the run-on end consonant. Unfortunately, the intrusive 'R' sound ('idea**R** of') is now appearing more and more in the middle of words: 'draw**Ring**' for 'drawing' and 'gnaw**Ring**' for 'gnawing'.

The hiatus between one word ending in a vowel and the next beginning with one, such as 'Anna and I', is often bridged - 'Ann**R**andI', and here, too, we get a run-on 'D' sound as well as the intrusive 'R'. An intrusive 'Y' sound is also to be avoided, as in 'I **Y**am happy.'

Why do so many actors fail to make themselves heard and understood today? In the 1950s, with the death of the well-made play and the drawing-room comedy, a reaction set in against Received Pronunciation. *The Beatles* made the Liverpool accent popular and an actor knew that he could get away with his own regional accent. In fact, he found that it was an advantage in the many parts that were being written for regional accents. Reaction against standard speech was found also in the schools and elocution became a dirty word. It was linked in many people's minds with artificiality and the 'how now, brown cow' approach.

But the time came when the actors with regional accents wished to play in Shakespeare, Shaw and Sheridan; in Chekov, Congreve and Wilde. They then realised that they were being asked to speak with Received Pronunciation. Even today, how-

34

ever, there is a school of thought which considers that this is not necessary. Because of the over-reaction to speech training, the baby has been thrown out with the bath water and the theatre is still suffering.

A contributing factor to the actor's inability to communicate is the increasing influence of television and the use of microphones. Actors who are used to working on television or radio often find it difficult to adjust their vocal technique to the vastly different demands of the stage. Additionally, I think that a misunderstanding of Stanislavski's method of acting is sometimes responsible for this failure to communicate. Actors have been encouraged to dig deep down inside themselves for their characters' psychological motivation, but they have not always been asked to convey the character's thoughts and feelings to the audience. Consequently, there have been performances when the actors not only failed to communicate with their audience but with their fellow members of the cast.

Because the actor's voice and speech are the tools of his trade it is necessary for him to keep them in perfect working order. Ten minutes a day spent on exercises should be enough to keep his vocal equipment in good trim. The value of this lies in the fact that it is a routine. Ten minutes a day, faithfully kept up, is of more benefit than an hour's session once a week.

Indistinct articulation is an even commoner reason for failure to communicate than lack of vocal power. However, projection is of vital importance too. This is not merely a question of using enough voice; there must also be a desire on the part of the actor to share his performance with everyone in the auditorium. It is a good idea to imagine that there is someone slightly deaf sitting in the back row of the stalls, the circles, pit and gallery.

Unfortunately, inaudibility and indistinctness seem to be on the increase in West End theatres today. Maybe the remedy lies with the audiences who, at present, suffer in silence. A few shouts of "Speak up!" from the back of the auditorium might work wonders!

An actor could have a perfectly produced voice, good enunciation and distinct articulation, but could still be a very bad performer, unless he was able to modulate his voice. Modulation is the expressive use of the voice and is allied to understanding, concentration, imagination and feeling. On the other hand, an actor could have all these qualities, but if he does not have the voice to express them, he could still fail. Therefore, he has first to create the instruments of voice and speech and then learn how to use them expressively.

James McKechnie was a fine radio actor. His voice was compelling. He was able to convey, apparently without effort, every nuance of meaning and every shade of emotion. I once asked him how he had acquired his technique - "I've never had a lesson in my life," he said. As well as his other qualities, he was born with naturally good voice production. Most of us have to work at it.

# Chapter Three

# Modulation

"It is not merely the thing that is said, but the man who says it that counts, the character which breathes through the sentences."

*Rosebery*

A child was asked what painting was. She considered a moment and then said "Well, I think and then I paint my think." Translated into terms of voice, that is what an actor should do. If one imagines a blank canvas as representing the lines which have to be spoken and the palette the artist holds as representing the different tones and shades of the voice; then, just as the artist's imagination enables him to select, mix and blend his colours, so should the actor's imagination enable him to modulate his voice to create a vivid picture in words.

There are various technical means of modulation which have to be mastered. The most obvious of these is a change of pitch. Few actors explore the full range of pitch in their voices. Laurence Olivier was a notable exception. I remember when he played Othello, I was surprised, knowing his voice as I did, to hear him speak the line,

"Keep up your bright swords, for the dew will rust them"

a full octave lower than I expected. He had added an octave to the top and bottom of his range for the part, through exercises. He was of course, a prodigious worker and always appreciated the value of keeping up voice exercises.

An useful exercise is to count on a spoken scale from ten down to one, trying to keep the intervals even, and then from one up to ten. People generally find it easier to work from the top down first. Number five should be regarded as the middle level of the pitch of the voice. Gradually work at achieving a higher note on ten and a lower one for one. The range of the voice will gradually be extended in this way, without forcing.

It is also an useful method of discovering where limitations in the voice lie. Some actors, particularly women, habitually pitch their voices too high. Think of the old-fashioned chest expander - a thick piece of elastic with a handle at each end. Imagine that you are gradually pulling the handles further and further apart. Once the exercise has been understood and practised it is useful, when studying a part, to pencil in a number or a tentative number at various points in a long speech as a guide to the level of pitch. The monotony which is caused by a too even use of pitch may then be avoided.

Naturally, the change of pitch should always be related to the meaning of the words and to the feeling behind them. Generally speaking, a change of subject or a new idea calls for a lift of pitch. But the speaker should be wary of starting each sentence on the same note and getting lower and lower. Not only will he be difficult to hear at the end of the phrase but he will also be liable to fall into a repetitive 'tune' in the voice, than which nothing is more boring.

A singer is sometimes described as having one or two good notes in the voice, but an uneven register. A speaker can favour one or two notes and keep returning to them, to the neglect of the rest of his range. When he is working at resonance exercises he should concentrate on the notes that he finds he is using least in performance. The control of pitch is essential in the speaking of long emotional speeches which rise to a climax. The usual mistake of many inexperienced actors is to go too high too early. When it comes to the climax at the end they have nothing more to give. With practice they can develop the ability to hold back the start of the build of the climax long enough to ensure that they have enough power to finish strongly. In a particularly difficult speech, such as Juliet's in the potion scene, control of the pitch is a crucial factor.

Here are some lines from *Henry V* which I find useful as a pitch exercise. It is a difficult one but effective in developing control. The numbered indications of pitch-levels are not necessarily the ones an actor would use in performance but are given to provide practice in building up and down from a climax.

| | |
|---|---|
| 5 | "and I know |
| 1 | 'Tis not the balm, the sceptre and the ball |
| 2 | The sword, the mace, the crown imperial |
| 3 | The intertissued robe of gold and pearl, |
| 4 | The farced title running fore the king, |
| 5 | The throne he sits on, (6) nor the tide of pomp |
| 7 | That beats upon the high shore of this world, |
| 8 | No, not all these, thrice-gorgeous ceremony |
| 9 | Not all these laid in bed majestical |
| 8 | Can sleep so soundly as the wretched slave |
| 7 | Who with a body fill'd and vacant mind |
| 6 | Gets him to rest cramm'd with distressful bread, |
| 5 | Never sees horrid night the child of hell, |
| 4 | But, like a lackey, from the rise to set |
| 3 | Sweats in the eye of Phoebus (2) and all night |
| 1 | Sleeps in Elysium." |

I have omitted the highest note in this as the exercise is quite taxing enough as it is. (1 represents the lowest note and 9 the highest.)

The following exercise is more suited to women, although either sex can use both this and the preceding one. The build up to the climax is easier in this exercise because the passage is shorter and does not demand so much sustained effort. It is from *A Midsummer Night's Dream*. This is not, of course, how one would treat it if actually playing the part of Titania. Again the start is on the middle pitch. The decasyllabic metre is convenient in providing a drop of pitch from ten down to one on the last line.

| | |
|---|---|
| 5 | "These are the forgeries of jealousy: |
| 1 | And never, since the middle summer's spring |
| 2 | Met we on hill, (3) in dale, (4) forest, (5) or mead, |
| 6 | By paved fountain, (7) or by rushy brook, |
| 8 | Or in the beached margent of the sea, |
| 9 | To dance our ringlets (10) to the whistling wind, |
| 10 | But (9) with (8) thy (7) brawls (6) thou (5) hast |
| | (4) dis (3) turb'd (2) our (1) sport." |

Purists might complain about lines from Shakespeare being used as exercises in this way. I find that his words stand up to the usage and, indeed, these two passages have never been spoilt for me, even though I have heard innumerable repetitions of them.

If an actor has a good ear for pitch he is not so likely to fall into the trap of catching the same pitch level of the actor who gives him his cue. Many plays begin with a long duologue. Particularly when the characters are the same sex, it is all too easy for them to catch each others' pitch of voice. One shuts one's eyes in the audience and is not always sure when one character has finished speaking and the next begins. It is necessary, too, for the director to have a keen ear, so that he can steer his cast away from this pitfall.

Change of pace is a valuable means of modulation, and an often neglected one. Laurence Olivier was once asked what acting was about and he replied succinctly, "Keeping the audience awake." Nothing lulls them to sleep more surely than an even pace and an even use of pitch.

What factors determine how fast an actor should speak? Obviously, the meaning of the words and the feeling behind them are the key elements; also the particular character that he is playing. It may be someone of mercurial vitality, young or old;

or a testy, choleric person. The physical state of the rôle will affect the pace as well, for example when drink is loosening the tongue.

From a technical point of view, the actor may be asked by the director to increase his pace in order to help build the scene to a climax or to support another character at a specific point in the play. How fast an actor speaks is governed by his powers of articulation. John Gielgud has always had the ability to speak rapidly without sacrificing distinctness.

Unless the lines are 'pointed', that is, unless the key words are brought out, rapid speech will become gabble. A definition of this word is useful to remember. "Gabble: voluble, confused unintelligible talk." Pace has been defined as the number of shots that can be put onto the target in a given time. But they must be accurate shots.

I sometimes hear amateur performances of plays in which the pace is set from beginning to end. Each new character making an entrance catches the prevailing tempo. This is disastrous when the first characters on are speaking too fast. The result is a breathless race towards the final curtain. It is more likely to happen in an one-act play than in a full-length play, during which someone may slow them down in the interval. However, a more sensible, medium pace has its dangers too as the audience may be lulled into a trance-like state. Even this is better than a too slow, even pace. Many a promising comedy has been ruined because of this. Changes of pace keep the audience alert, help in shaping the play to its major and minor climaxes and help the actors to sustain interest in their long speeches.

A sudden injection of speed can be exciting: one is carried along by the exuberant vitality as when listening to the faster passages in Benjamin Britten's compositions. Modulation of the voice in acting is closely related to music. But the actor has not the same guidelines such as notes and bars and indications of tempi. A playwright is not so specific in his demands as a composer. Therefore, although an actor may have more freedom in the use of pitch and pace, he has also more licence to go wrong. Additionally, a composer will also indicate, the amount of volume he requires, but the actor usually has to work this out for himself.

The third means of modulation to be considered is voice amount. A speaker is capable of producing varying levels of sound, ranging from a whisper to a shout. At the extremities of this range, technical problems may arise. Actors who have to shout a good deal in a production sometimes lose their voices. They become worried and the condition grows worse. It is essential that the voice is not forced and that the throat-muscles are not constrained. The pitch should not be allowed to become too high. There is a tendency now for actors to use too loud a volume for too long. A little shouting goes a long way. If overdone, it will batter the ears of the audience until, in self-defence, they stop listening. Another disadvantage of overdoing shouting is that it tends to make the characters sound alike, because it is more difficult to colour the tone when the sound is increased. Properly used, shouting can convey a great range of emotions, including triumph, despair, anger, astonishment, fear, indignation and horror.

A very soft delivery of lines has to be carefully controlled. Many speakers equate a quiet voice with a breathy one. When speaking quietly, it is important to support the voice with good breath-control, so that the resonance is not lost.

In the old fairground days there was a side show in which ping-pong balls danced about on the top of jets of water. The aim was to perforate the celluloid by shooting at them. The water entered the holes and caused the ping-pong balls to drop. So, if the breath is represented by the jets of water and the voice by the ping-pong balls, one can see the importance of supporting the voice by breath and not allowing the breath to come into the tone. When a stage-whisper is used, the reverse applies: no voice should be allowed to enter the breathy tone. In both these examples the use of the abdominal press is a vital technique.

In addition to changes of pitch, pace and voice amount, modulation embraces all forms of emphasis. An entire book could be devoted to the subject of emphatic values. When an actor uses a false emphasis one suspects that he has not studied his lines sufficiently or that he misunderstands them. Emphasis is the bringing of a certain word or words in a phrase, the key words, into prominence. There are ten different ways of doing this but few people make use of more than two or three of them.

The three main means of modulation already mentioned can be used. *Change of pitch* is an extreme method, employed more often in Restoration and Wildean comedy, than anywhere else. A famous example was Edith Evans' treatment of "A handbag" in *The Importance of Being Earnest*. A sudden *change of pace* from fast or medium to slow, or vice versa, can also be effective as is a sudden increase or decrease in *voice amount*. If an actor feels that he is losing the attention of his audience and starts to speak in a very quiet voice, he will often be able to make them listen again as they then have to concentrate in order to hear what he is saying. He should, of course, be just audible.

Of the remaining forms of emphasis the most common, and least subtle, is to use *added stress*. It is necessary to say added stress because words of more than one syllable in English already carry a stress. This method of emphasis is favoured by many a politician in election speeches. But the law of diminishing returns then comes into operation. The audience will listen to him at first but the continuous battering of their ears by hammer blows of sound will cause them to switch off, metaphorically and literally, if the speech is being delivered on radio or television.

A far more subtle way of bringing words into prominence is by the use of *inflection*. This is the glide of the voice within the pitch. It is sometimes referred to by examination candidates as 'infliction' (which it may be if misused) or, more recently, as 'inflation'. Its primary function is to bring out meaning and it is an effective way of giving significance to a word. A rising, falling, circumflex or compound inflection may be used:

I absolutely refuse to do that, *or*

I absolutely refuse to do that, *or*

I absolutely refuse to do that, *or*

I absolutely refuse to do that.

A neglected way of bringing out a key word is to use *pause*. A resourceful actor can use it in three different ways to point a line. He can pause before the word,

"I suspect that he / forged the document."

He can pause after the operative word, to let its full implication sink in,

"What she said was treasonable / and she cannot be allowed to go."

If he wishes to make a point very strongly indeed, he can pause both before and after the word, isolating it in the sentence,

"We have reached / deadlock / in these negotiations."

Care must be taken, however, when an actor is speaking blank verse, not to extend these pauses so long as to disturb the rhythm of the lines unduly nor to suggest that he has forgotten his lines.

Yet another means of giving significance is by the use of *intensity*. Intensity can be dramatically effective. The technique is to reduce volume and to produce the voice with considerable nervous pressure behind it. It is allied to restraint. You could compare it to the forcible emission of steam from a pressure cooker when the temperature inside has been raised sufficiently. It calls for the control of the speaker's outgoing breath by means of the abdominal press. It is an useful means of conveying a profoundly emotional state, as in the following phrase from *Othello*,

"Villain, be sure thou prove my love a whore."

The tenth means of emphasis is *movement*. An actor may bang the table to make a point. But, obviously, he should not bang it on the actual word he wants to bring out. If he does he will drown it. It is safer to make the gesture immediately before.

I have dwelt at some length on the various means of achieving emphasis because they are such a useful part of the actor's craft. Edith Evans was a past-mistress in the art of judging emphatic values and in their selective use. A stage-manager friend told me a story about her which may, or may not, be apocryphal, illustrating Dame Edith's conscientious approach. She was rehearsing in a West End theatre and during the lunch break she was sitting in the wings with her sandwiches and going over her lines while the rest of the company had gone out to lunch. The stage-manager of the company was working with one of the resident stage crew when they heard the following projected loudly and clearly into the empty auditorium in Dame Edith's inimitable tones,

"WHAT do men want?
What DO men want?
What do MEN want?
What do men WANT?"
"Oh for gawd's sake miss go and tell her what it is men want."

Good modulation implies the marriage of sound and sense. A musical voice may actually be a disadvantage to an actor, as the sound may distract attention from what he is saying. Sir John Gielgud has sometimes been accused of letting the music of his voice obscure the sense. I have never subscribed to this criticism. His keen intellect shines through all that he does and I do not think that he has ever been guilty of using a false emphasis.

Sometimes drama students, finding that they have acquired strong, flexible voices, fall into the habit of listening to themselves speak. What emerges is a meaningless wash of sound. One cure is to give them dialogue which is witty and astringent and to avoid working on anything lyrical.

When an actor puts his imagination, concentration and his heart and mind behind a well-produced voice he achieves tone-colour. Some actors, it is true, are born with such an emotive quality in the voice that they could move one even if they were reading from the telephone directory. The French have a descriptive phrase for it - *larmes dans la voix*. Both Sarah Bernhardt and Ellen Terry were gifted in this way: Sarah Bernhardt with her "golden voice" and Ellen Terry with a voice which James Agate described as being "like the heart of a red rose." Every actor, whether blessed with this kind of voice or not, can, with determination and practice, acquire tone-colour.

Once the techniques of modulation have been mastered, the voice should respond instinctively to the demands of the script. I once heard Marius Goring reading Tennyson's *Maud* with dazzling virtuosity. One knew that his vocal technique was so secure, that his mind was free to interpret what he was reading. Gielgud demonstrated the evocative power of tone-colour particularly effectively as Caesar speaking to the Sphinx in the opening scene of Shaw's *Caesar and Cleopatra*:

> "In the little world yonder, Sphinx, my place is as high as yours is in *this great desert.*"

What vast, unpeopled, timeless spaces were conjured up by the way he said those last three words. I wondered how many shovels of sand would have to be thrown on the stage, what clever lighting used to suggest the distances which the actor was able to suggest by his voice alone. Once an actor's vocal technique is secure, to think and to communicate the thought expressively should become an immediate and instinctive process.

I do not need to expand upon the importance of keeping the voice in good trim, particularly during a long run of a play and when the part makes unusual demands on the voice, such as when the character has to sing. I am told by singers who perform in Gilbert and Sullivan that the alternation between spoken and sung words is very taxing.

A daily routine of relaxation, breathing and voice exercises is essential in these circumstances and, indeed, to be recommended throughout an actor's career, whatever part he is playing. The human voice, properly used, will stand up to heavy demands and may, indeed, benefit from them. Many of our leading actors have retained their vocal power and expressiveness well into old age.

To illustrate the means of modulation described in this chapter, I have chosen some passages of prose and verse. However, I have mainly chosen verse because, as it is a heightened form of expression, it makes more demands on the speaker in a shorter space of time than prose does.

A sensuous poet like John Keats demands warmth of tone, as in these words from *Ode to a Nightingale* in which he describes the bird as a "light-winged Dryad of the Trees" who "singest of Summer with full-throated ease." The long vowel sounds of 'OH' and 'EE' are helpful to the speaker here.

The actor should take note of adjectives. These give him a clue as to how to colour the words. There is a phrase in Matthew Arnold's *Dover Beach* which calls for subtle tone-colouring:

> "the cliffs of England stand
> Glimmering and vast, out in the tranquil bay."

Nine speakers out of ten will make no difference in the way they speak those two adjectives. The only way to evoke the necessary atmosphere is to imagine the glimmer of the white chalk cliffs and then their size whilst saying the lines.

I am always struck by the sudden appearance of this lyrical passage in Robert Burns' robust narrative poem *Tam O'Shanter*. After his description of the cronies boozing in the tavern, he waxes philosophical,

> "But pleasures are like poppies spread -
> You seize the flow'r its bloom is shed
> Or like the snow falls in the river -
> A moment white then melts for ever."

All the coaching and technique in the world will not help the speaker to catch the atmosphere of these words unless he imagines a snow flake alighting on the surface of the water and resting there for a fleeting moment. If he does, he will almost certainly use a quiet voice, a light touch and a slight lift of pitch.

I have heard verse-speaking described as an old-fashioned way of training an actor. But I believe it to be of immense value, providing of course that the sound is not allowed to swamp the sense of the words.

Turning to dramatic verse, in these lines from *Macbeth*,

> "Light thickens, and the crow
> Makes wing to th' rooky wood;
> Good things of day begin to drop and drowse,
> While night's black agents to their preys do rouse."

Again the voice may be used quietly, but this time there is much more weight behind the words. Macbeth has just planned the murder of Banquo and Fleance and his superstitious fear of night is darkening his mind. Obviously, the pitch will be lower, the pace slower, the vocal texture quite different from that demanded by the Burns quotation.

Changes of pace are valuable when speaking Shakespeare as they break up what could be the steady and monotonous march of the iambic feet. A change of pace is clearly indicated in Puck's speech in the last act of *A Midsummer Night's Dream*,

> "Now it is the time of night
> That the graves, all gaping wide,
> Everyone lets forth his sprite,
> In the church-way paths to glide
> And we fairies that do run
> By the triple Hecate's team
> From the presence of the sun,
> Following darkness like a dream
> Now are frolic . . ."

I have sometimes seen Puck illustrating this speech by vigorous movement on every line. But Shakespeare has conveyed the atmosphere in the words. Again, it is a question of concentrating the mind on the picture that the words conjure up. If the actor does this he should have no difficulty with the modulation. He will naturally use a deeper, slower delivery for the first four lines and a lighter, quicker one for the following five.

I have mentioned the 'march' of the iambic feet and the need to avoid monotony. However, Shakespeare sometimes makes deliberate use of the regular alternation of stressed and unstressed syllables. In *King John,* the distraught Constance describes her state of mind when her young son Arthur has been imprisoned in the Tower,

> "Grief fills the room up of my absent child,
> Lies in his bed, walks up and down with me."

The restless pacing of someone in unbearable distress may be suggested by the steady pace here.

In *Romeo and Juliet*, the forward movement of a standard bearer is suggested by the regularity of the metre in Romeo's speech at the end of the play as he looks at Juliet and says,

> ". . . beauty's Ensign yet
> Is crimson in thy lips and in thy cheeks,
> And death's / pale flag / is not / ad / vanced there."

A steady delivery of this line heightens the implied image of movement across a battlefield.

Strongly emotional speeches which build to a big climax are difficult to control. One needs to exercise restraint at the beginning as regards increase of volume. It is here that intensity is useful, as in these lines from *Julius Caesar*, when Mark Antony is left alone on the stage, mourning over Caesar's body. To begin with a mood of sombre prophecy is the key-note,

> "Domestic fury and fierce civil strife
> Shall cumber all the parts of Italy;
> Blood and destruction shall be so in use,
> And dreadful objects so familiar,
> That mothers shall but smile when they behold
> Their infants quartered with the hands of war,
> All pity chok'd with custom of fell deeds."

Then the actor can afford to let go vocally as he works up to the big climax of,

> "And Caesar's spirit, ranging for revenge,
> With Ate by his side come hot from hell,
> Shall in these confines with a Monarch's voice
> Cry 'Havoc' and let slip the dogs of war."

The final two lines of the speech could either be sustained on the same note (difficult, technically, to bring off successfully) or the pitch could be lowered and the words given a charged feeling of prophetic horror:

> "That this foul deed shall smell above the earth
> With carrion men, groaning for burial."

A sensitive actor should be able to convey, the exact shades of meaning and shifts of feeling that the lines demand, through a flexible use of the voice. And, of course, the imagination must be involved.

Many players are capable of deep feeling, but fewer of giving it full expression. They allow the emotion to strangle and choke the utterance and their genuine emotional response is not communicated to their listeners. In the following two lines of Gerard Manley Hopkins, the obvious tenderness has to be judged exactly in terms of the sound produced,

"Because the Holy Ghost over the bent
World broods with warm breast and with ah bright Wings!"

To add to the difficulty here there is a change of feeling on "and with ah bright Wings" which calls for a change in the tone-colour.

So far my illustrations have been fairly explicit lines. However, today's playwrights tend not to write in this way. The subtext has to be explored in order for the correct colour to be given to the words. This is particularly true of the dialogue of Harold Pinter and Alan Bennett.

The Duchess in *Alice's Adventures in Wonderland* advised Alice to "Take care of the sense, and the sounds will take care of themselves." This maxim cannot be applied to Pinteresque dialogue. Beneath the apparently conversational style yawn depths of feeling, passion even. One should perhaps say "Take care of the *feeling* and the sounds will take care of themselves." In a famous speech from *The Caretaker*, Aston describes how he was given electric-shock treatment incorrectly in a mental hospital. He describes what happened to him afterwards, how he could "never quite get it together." At the end of the speech he says,

"I've often thought of going back and trying to find the man who did that to me."

Underneath the apparently casual words there is a terrible menace which has to be conveyed. A quiet tone is needed but it has to be coloured with the memory of all that he has suffered at the hands of that doctor and also with the thought of what he would do to him if he met him again.

A change to a slow pace is useful when a performer wishes to sum up what has gone before, to gather together the experience of a whole speech or poem, as in the first line of the last verse of Dylan Thomas' *And Death Shall Have No Dominion*. It is the fifth time that Thomas has used this line. Repetition makes great demands on the speaker's powers of modulation. The line this time has to be spoken in a way which suggests a mood of reassurance and triumph. So, although the pace is slow, a major tone should enter the voice,

"And death shall have no dominion."

And when, in the middle of Sassoon's exuberant ending to *Concert Interpretation,*

"Lynch the conductor! Jugulate the drums!
Butcher the brass! Ensanguinate the strings!
Throttle the flutes! . . . "

he suddenly changes the mood to

" . . . Stravinsky's April comes
With pitiless pomp and pain of sacred springs"

a slowing down of the pace will give the necessary processional quality to the words.

The authorised version of *The Bible* demands a sensitive ear in order for the reader to respond to the rapid changes of mood. *Revelation,* Chapter 21, verses 1 to 8 are a good test of bible-reading. First there is a sense of wonder,

"And I John saw the Holy City, new Jerusalem,
coming down from God out of heaven,
prepared as a bride adorned for her husband."

Then follows the "great voice out of heaven" and what it promises mankind. The compassion of,

"And God shall wipe away all tears from their eyes,
and there shall be no more death neither sorrow,
nor crying, neither shall there be any more pain"

must be felt and conveyed. A passage of affirmation comes next and immediately afterwards, one of threatening doom,

"But the fearful, and unbelieving, and the abominable and
murderers, and whoremongers, and sorcerers and idolaters,
and all liars, shall have their part in the lake which burneth
with fire and brimstone which is the second death."

Very few readers manage to suggest all these changes of mood in the voice and with subtlety - bible-reading should *never* be dramatised.

For some reason, the expression of positive and cheerful states of mind seems to be more difficult than the expression of unhappy ones. Uncertainty, sorrow or despair are usually more effectively conveyed by the speaking voice than gladness, joy or ecstasy. This thought crossed my mind when I was listening to a recording of the glorious sound of Kirsten Flagstadt in Act Two of *Tristan and Isolde* which celebrates the ecstasy of the lovers. This radiance is harder to achieve in a speaking voice because the higher notes are more difficult to control than the lower ones and have less resonance.

Simple exercises can be used to build up confidence, even when a performer has to express ecstasy. In the following example (rather a descent from *Tristan and Isolde*, I'm afraid!), the statements of extreme gloom gradually brighten into euphoria,

> "It's Monday morning.
> It's pouring with rain.
> The clouds are lifting.
> It's stopped raining.
> Here comes the postman.
> A letter for me.
> I've won the pools!"

Then the rapture gradually fades into the light of common day,

> "I've won the pools
> It's not a bad dividend.
> Not as much as I'd hoped.
> It's starting to rain.
> The clouds are getting blacker.
> It's raining cats and dogs.
> It's Monday morning."

Complex states of mind are difficult to convey. Strindberg has given Miss Julie a speech in which she is trying to urge Christine to go abroad with her and Jean to start a new life. Her feverish vitality, covering great distress, can be shown by the adoption of an artificial brightness of tone, a false cheerfulness which falters and drops on certain phrases into devitalised sadness. She speaks more and more slowly until the flat delivery of the last words,

"And then we can come back here -
or somewhere else."

When self-pity is avoided this is one of the most moving speeches in the play.

A knowledge of technique will help actors to solve most of the problems of modulation which they encounter. However, it is noticeable that these problems often do not arise for very young performers. They are just not aware of them. Once, I was adjudicating at a Speech and Drama Festival and watching a scene from *Peter Pan* acted by two eight-year olds. It was the scene in the Darling Nursery between Peter and Wendy - Peter was being played by a girl. The light, clear voice of Wendy contrasted perfectly with the assumed, deeper, gruffish tones of Peter. All the changes of mood were naturally and clearly communicated. Pitch, pace and voice amount were all varied. I am sure that, while both children had obviously been well taught, they had not been initiated into the techniques of modulation. They acted with the vivid imagination and true feeling of the very young. The young Peter and Wendy were completely relaxed. They saw and felt the situation through the vividness of their imagination and their voices reflected what their minds pictured. The conductor of a youth orchestra has said that he was amazed by the way that the young instrumentalists flew over difficulties in the score without realising that they were there. They would, of course, be helped by a relaxed approach.

Actors have to be able to recapture this imaginative approach. Although the powerful imagination of childhood weakens in most people as they grow older, actors have to practice to keep this faculty fresh and strong. Improvisation is an useful method of doing so. An actor can, through emotional recall, go back to past incidents in his life and rekindle the fires of the imagination. William Wordsworth has already described it all in his *Ode on the Intimations of Immortality*.

However, technique cannot be ignored. A mature actor may have vivid powers of imagination and concentration, but if he has not the voice and the mastery of modulation to put his thought and feeling over to the audience, his efforts will be wasted.

# Chapter Four

# Movement

"Suit the action to the word, the word to the action."
*Hamlet*

*Movement* involves an actor's use of his body, from the slightest flicker of an eyelash to a sweeping gesture, from a couple of hesitant steps, to a run across the stage. It is a great pity that movement is all too often compartmentalised during an actor's training. He has classes in dance, period movement, classical, modern jazz and tap. He has classes in mime. But not one seems to be sufficiently related to the kind of movement he needs when he is bringing a character to life visually, on the stage. Consequently one sees students who move beautifully in a dance class, but are unable to put one foot in front of another naturally in a play.

However, the situation is now changing because of the emergence of musical theatre in which performers are required to dance, act and sing equally well. There is beginning to be more integration of these expressive arts in drama schools.

But the technique of stage movement is often neglected in training. Actors who have been through drama school should know the most natural way to turn on the stage, and yet how often they go the long way round. So much depends on footwork in acting and knowing on which foot to carry the weight. And yet some arrive at their first professional engagement seemingly unaware of this elementary technique. It should be assimilated early on in training and then forgotten, because it has become instinctive. It is too late to start learning it, by trial and error, during performances in front of a paying public.

The few basic rules of stage movement, which of course can be broken, provide a secure basis. Rules are often sneered at, just as examinations are. I remember saying to my father "I don't hold with examinations." "Maybe not", he replied drily, "but pass them."

It is wise to learn the rules of stage technique. Then, if he breaks them, the actor will do so deliberately and know what he is doing. There is sound commonsense behind most of them. For instance, if the actor kneels on the downstage knee, the one nearer to the audience, he opens up his shoulders and his face can be seen from all parts of the auditorium. But if he kneels on the upstage one he is in danger of presenting three-quarters of his back to a third of the audience. I saw this happen recently in a West End production, in a scene in which it was vital that we saw the character's facial expression. Directors should not let this happen. However, it is ultimately the actor's responsibility to be aware of this basic technique.

While there may be impatience in the profession with any insistence on commonsense rules of movement, there is a surprising adherence, even among seasoned actors, to old-fashioned dogma, for instance - you must never turn your back on the audience. In some amateur dramatic societies this rule is taken as gospel.

I can understand the reason for the obsession among two groups of performers - ballet dancers and opera singers. Both have to be weaned away, when they are acting, from the idea that there is a conductor in the orchestra pit. Even when they are in a play, students who have had ballet training tend to turn their heads rapidly round if they are, reluctantly, positioned with their backs to the audience. Those who have had training in opera have a tendency to play everything out front to the auditorium.

An actor can express a great deal with his back. Alfred Lunt, a fine American actor, was renowned for his eloquent back view. This was so characteristic of his style that, when he and Lynne Fontanne returned to London after a lapse of some years, the drama critic of a national newspaper headed his review with the words *Alfred Lunt's Back*.

Performers in Gilbert and Sullivan and in early musical comedies were in the habit of playing square on to the audience, but styles are changing. More straight-acting technique is demanded in the genres of opera, Gilbert and Sullivan and musicals.

Actors have to be versatile; the lines of demarcation between musicals and straight plays are becoming shadowy. However, although their acting technique is useful to them when they are playing in a musical, straight actors have to modify their style, particularly as regards movement and positioning. Robert Lindsay achieved this brilliantly in the revival of *Me and My Girl*. His acting, singing and dancing were integrated into a convincing, sustained characterisation which critics were quick to appreciate, both in London and on Broadway.

To come back to footwork. Alec Guinness complained that a remark of his about building up his characters from the feet and the walk is always being quoted. It is not surprising, though, that such a useful aid to characterisation is so often referred to. I am sure that other actors use it too. Gielgud must surely have drawn some of the inspiration for his creation of the bar-fly Spooner in Pinter's *No Man's Land* from the sandshoes he wore early on in rehearsal. The height of the heel affects the way a person stands and walks and so all through rehearsals it is wise to wear shoes which are appropriate to the character.

Many actors find it surprisingly difficult to walk across the stage naturally. This apparently simple exercise brings out a strained self-consciousness in even the experienced. Some are able to do it effortlessly. Felicity Kendal made a move across the stage in Stoppard's *The Real Thing* which was a miracle of seemingly artless naturalness and grace. More recently, in Simon Gray's *Hidden Laughter*, her movement demonstrated an effortless mastery of technique.

Footwork presents formidable problems to many young players. Either they look as if their feet are nailed to the stage so that they are unable to move from one spot, or they shift their weight nervously from foot to foot, or they may creep around the stage in an aimless way. This is usually because they are insufficiently motivated: they have not got a strong enough reason for the move.

On the whole, inexperienced actors tend to use too much movement and gesture, rather than too little. A good way of working, in order to achieve a clear-cut performance, is to start in rehearsal by putting everything in as the feeling prompts one and then, gradually, to take out every superficial, unnecessary movement, every ineffectual repetition, until one is left with the minimum that is required to convey character, feeling and motive to the audience.

It is useful to think of a cartoonist who might start with a detailed, complete picture and then gradually take out all the unnecessary lines until he is left with an outline - an economical expression of what he wants to say. To boil it down to practicalities: do not use four hand movements when two would do.

Nina's remark, "I know I am acting abominably, I don't know what to do with my hands", in *The Seagull* draws, I am sure, a sympathetic response from many. I remember one student who had particular difficulty. I told him that his hands were like bunches of bananas. We worked together for a term, at the end of which he asked "Are my hands any better now?" "Yes, they are now mobile bunches of bananas." I saw him the other day acting in the West End. His body, arms and hands were fluently expressive. His is by no means an unusual problem. Hands and arms and what to do with them present great difficulties to actors. However, through training, and at the start of their careers in the profession, there are several ways of surmounting the problem.

Exercises in mime, concentrating on the movement of shoulders, arms, wrists and fingers help to free the muscles. There is a sequence which Marcel Marceau created in which he mimed the catching of a butterfly, dropping it on the ground, picking it up, apparently lifeless, and coaxing it back to life, which largely depends on the movement of the fingers. One can start by practising simple exercises in occupational mime, such as opening a box of matches and striking a match, or tying and untying a shoe lace. To be of any value, they have to be done with precision and truth.

Another workshop session could be used for practising pouring out drinks and swallowing them. An untasted or hardly sipped glass of spirits is noticed by the audience, especially when the character appears to be getting drunk. For all everyday actions - reading a newspaper, smoking, drinking - the actor has examples all around him. He can observe the different ways in which commuters handle their morning and evening newspapers, how people hold glasses and tankards in the pub or at a party. The way a person smokes a cigarette is character-revealing.

Stage properties are often lighter than the objects they represent. The actor, therefore, has to imagine and mime the weight of the real thing. This is particularly necessary in Shakespeare because the props include goblets, drinking vessels of all kinds, crowns, battle-axes and swords. One often sees 'gold' goblets containing liquid airily lifted. Care should be taken in the handling of suitcases. In no less than four recent productions in the West End suitcases were carried on, apparently empty, although they were, presumably, supposed to be full of clothes. The stage management cannot always be relied on to weight stage luggage.

If substitute props are provided as soon as the actors know their lines, are 'off the book', detailed and accurate miming of the weight can be practised and then, when it comes to the performance, the handling of these props should be convincing.

While we are on the subject of miming, thought can be given to the tricky business of writing letters on the stage. It is patently absurd when a character makes a few perfunctory scratches with a pen and then proceeds to read out the long sentence he has, supposedly, just written. Some artistic license must be granted as, obviously, when writing a long letter the actor cannot take the actual time that he would in real life. But the audience's credulity should not be strained. A good exercise is provided by Marjorie Pinchwife's letter-writing scene in Wycherley's *The Country Wife*. It is probably easier to manage if she is seen to scribble one or two phrases hastily, before reading them out aloud. The word by word method becomes tedious.

Personal props such as gloves, sticks, cigarette cases and umbrellas can present unforeseen difficulties. A lighter which refuses to function, an umbrella which will not open, gloves which cannot be pulled on or off - these are all parts of an actor's nightmares.

A most unfortunate sequence of mishaps occurred in a scene during the performance of a Victorian play I was in. The villain of the piece was the victim. First, the hook of his cloak, which he had left on the table, caught on the lace table-runner and when he went to pick it up, the runner was whirled in a parabola through the air, catching and displacing one side of his false moustache as it went. When he was about to make a dramatic exit, clapping his top hat on, he miscalculated the height of the door and this caused the hat to be jammed down over one eye. It was not surprising then, that he tripped up the steps leading from the basement room to the street. It was a scene which might have been described by Michael Green in his book, *The Art of Coarse Acting*. I can still remember the herculean effort it took to keep a straight face whilst I was watching this!

This kind of accident can always happen and is almost impossible to guard against. However, rehearsals with personal properties can usually familiarise an actor with any hazards which may crop up in performance, or at least mitigate disastrous results.

## The Representation of Age

*"For Age, with stealing steps,*
*Hath clawed me with his clutch"*
Lord Vaux

Young actors frequently play very old characters convincingly. They seem to find this easier than the representation of middle age. The mistake that most of us have made, in youth, is to play any character over fifty as if senile decay had already set in.

Again, observation is the answer to many of the technical difficulties involved in moving like a middle-aged or elderly person. Examples of every age from babyhood onwards are around us every day. The check-out desk at a supermarket is an excellent place at which to observe the way people of different ages use their hands, when they are getting out their money to pay. The old and infirm struggle with arthritic fingers to find the coins. You see the casual grace of the movements of a young girl and so on. I am fascinated, in another context, by watching how babies use their hands and fingers. They provide an object lesson in relaxed, unself-conscious movement. Their emotions are instantly communicated by the way they bunch their fists, stretch their fingers, use their thumbs.

A good exercise in observation is to ask a group of students to imagine that they are babies in a crêche. You can pick out at once those who base their movement on observation and truth and those who base it on a clichéd, stereotyped idea of babyhood.

When representing old age it is useful to remember that people tend to shrink in height. Ankles and knee-joints are affected, old peoples feet tend to be turned out when they are walking and sitting. If this is remembered, the conventional picture of 'stage old-age', of a person hobbling about, leaning forward on a stick will be seen to be false.

One sometimes sees a performance of old age which is convincing from the waist down. But the flexible movement of the shoulders and neck gives the game away. The head tends to come forward in old age, the neck muscles and the shoulder-joints stiffen and the movement of the neck, shoulders and upper arms is restricted.

Small boys of eight, nine and ten can sometimes produce such astonishingly accurate portrayals of old men that, if the scenery were scaled down to their size and if they were in the appropriate costume and make-up, they would be entirely convincing, visually. This is the result of imagination, concentration, observation and their ability to relax on the stage. They become the thing that their imagination sees.

## The Angle of the Head

I had never thought about the angle of the head in acting until Athene Seyler gave me a short, but never to be forgotten, lesson in her dressing-room at the Savoy. She seized my chin firmly in her hand and moved it in various directions. She made me look in the mirror to see for myself the effect that different angles could produce. She taught me that an oblique position is more interesting than one directly facing the audience or in profile to it.

The angle of the head naturally affects the eye-level. There is an enormous range of possibilities here which is seldom fully explored. Some actors 'dodge' the 'fourth wall' and all the audience ever sees of them is the profile. Some actors look down too much and lose a valuable asset. The eyes are the most expressive feature of the face and eyes are more interesting to look at than eyelids.

One should judge the angle of the head very carefully when looking up. If you tilt the head back and look directly up at the supposed sky or ceiling your eyes may not be seen at all, or only the whites of them. The same thing may happen if your focal point is too near the front of the stage. But if you tilt the head so that you are looking up at an angle of about forty-five degrees, and your focal point is out front, your facial expression will be seen fully and, moreover, you will not be straining your neck muscles.

## The Effect of Temperature on Movement

It is no good wearing tropical clothes and greasing the face to suggest sweat if the movement does not show the lassitude and discomfort caused by extreme heat. And the movement must be consistent. Suddenly fanning the face and sinking into a chair, saying "Phew, it's a scorcher today" does not carry conviction if the actor's movements in the rest of the scene have been vigorous. He has to recall what it felt like in real life when he was unbearably hot, and how this affected him physically.

It is probably easier to suggest that one is extremely cold, but a perfunctory stretching out of the hands to a fire or heater is not enough. The actor has to recollect the discomfort of frozen feet and icy fingertips and ears. All the ingenuity of the stage-management in showing ice, snow and blizzard conditions through the window, all the detailed effects of snow on boots and shoulders will be wasted if the actor does not show he is cold by his movement.

## Movement in Period Plays

Whatever the period, the costume will affect deportment, walk and gesture. The weight and line of the costume are two vital considerations and, of course, the type of footwear. Equally important is the knowledge of what was worn underneath the costume.

Clichés abound in period plays. One of these is the curious idea that all females in Victorian society tripped along winsomely instead of walking. This unnatural gait is not confined to amateurs, it sometimes finds its way into professional productions as well. It is worth remembering Edith Evans' remark that "I find the life in the character and then put it into its period." Contemporary accounts of fashionable life are a valuable source of information. *The Exercise of the Fan* by Joseph Addison gives a detailed account of the use of the fan in the late seventeenth and early eighteenth centuries:

"To unfurl the fan is to open it by degrees, again to shut it, and to make it assume coquettish undulations in the process. To discharge the fan is to open it all at once, so as to make a little rustling noise which attracts the attention of those absorbed young men who neglect to ogle you. To ground the fan is to set it down, no matter where, while pretending to readjust a curl...To flutter the fan is to cool the face with it. There is an infinite variety of motions to be made use of in the flutter of a fan: there is the angry flutter; the modest flutter; the timorous flutter; the merry flutter; and the amorous flutter. Not to be tedious, there is scarce any emotion in the mind which does not produce a suitable agitation in the fan."

Correct period style can be studied too in paintings and fashion-plates and in early photographs. I have a particularly useful picture of a Wagner family party in 1880. There are numerous good books on costume. *A Concise History of Costume* by James Laver has lavish illustrations of the Victorian period. During the sixty-four years of Victoria's reign the size of the skirt developed from the expanding one which was achieved by wearing more and more petticoats underneath to the '*cage crinoline*' which appeared in 1856. About 1860 it was at its widest. Gradually, the crinoline began to slip to the back and became, eventually, a kind of bustle. These changes in costume present different problems to the wearer: how to come through the door in a very wide crinoline; how to sit down gracefully without allowing it to spring up revealing, at best, pantaloons or, at worst, modern panties.

Men's costume altered less spectacularly during this period, although the height of the collar increased. Upright posture showed off the line of the frock coat. Trousers were narrow and strapped under the instep. Movement was restricted because the morning coat was buttoned high over the chest.

Moving well in period costume is not just a matter of wearing the clothes confidently. The actor has to think himself back into the social and moral climate of the time. This will affect everything that he does from drinking tea and conversing with the opposite sex, to comporting himself on formal, public occasions.

The appropriate underclothes will not only give women's costumes the correct line but will make the performer feel right. And even when the detail of make-up is not seen by the audience it helps the actor. When Sarah Bernhardt was playing Cleopatra, she painted her nails. "But no-one will see them from the audience", someone said to her. "I shall see them", she replied.

It is not only in the movement that clichés are to be found in period plays. They can also be found in the costumes. That delicious pastiche, Sandy Wilson's *The Boy Friend,* has had an unfortunate effect on straight plays set in the 1920s. Costumes have been exaggerated and the movement over-stylised. The short skirts of the period throw emphasis on the legs and the amusing, mannered positions of the girls in *The Boy Friend* cannot be imitated in a straight play without making the characters seem unreal. Incidentally, Vida Hope, who directed that musical, told me that the quartet of girls were, in her view, the key to its success. She had taken care in rehearsals to catch the slightly exaggerated 1920s period look and movement appropriate for this pastiche.

However, for a straight play, set in the twenties and thirties it is safer to go to photographs, old newspapers and magazines of the period and thus avoid the risk of the clichéd movement which might result in imitating the style of *The Boy Friend.*

## Why Do I Move?

This question is often asked by students in training. There should always be a reason, a motivation for a movement. If a director gives a move for which there is no apparent reason, the actor himself should try to create a motive for it. Otherwise it will be, and will look like, 'a director's move' and will not carry conviction. A motive may vary in strength from the desire to attack another character physically, to the need to open the window to let in some fresh air. There are one or two guidelines which are useful to bear in mind. A movement towards another character heightens tension; a movement away, reduces tension. Some students have a habit of taking a step or two backwards when they are addressing an imaginary character in an audition speech. This type of movement weakens dramatic impact and should only be used when emotions such as uncertainty, fear or cowardice are being conveyed.

There is a movement which always reminds me of someone stepping out of a chorus line. This is when only one step forward is taken. Again, observation of the way in which people move in real life is necessary. That kind of artificial movement would only be seen in particular circumstances: following an explicit command to take one step forward, for instance. In addition, observation will show that when most people get up from a chair or sofa they do not remain standing close to it.

Sitting does present some difficulties. An actor should note and remember the exact position of a chair so that he does not have to turn round to see where it is before sitting down. This looks as if he is suspicious of the stage-management's efficiency in placing the furniture, especially if it is during a scene after a change of setting. Some people find it reassuring to feel the edge of the chair with the back of the knee before lowering themselves onto the seat. Casual dashes at furniture can be dangerous - actors have been known to miss the arm of a chair completely. I once neglected to make sure that a footstool had been placed in its usual position in front of the fireplace, in a period play, and sat down on nothing revealing a considerable expanse of leg.

Entrances and exits have to be carefully timed, particularly when the character has to enter at speed. An actor's first entrance is vitally important as it is then that the audience's attention is fully on him. Character has to be established immediately. For most it is necessary to concentrate on getting into the part for a few minutes before making an entrance, but an experienced player may be able to plunge into his character, even if he has been chatting in the wings a moment before.

The same applies to orchestral players if this story, told to me by John Pashby of Sotheby's is anything to go by:

"Many years ago I was invited by Sir (then Mr.) John Barirolli to sit in the orchestra for a performance of *Die Meistersinger* at Streatham Hill Theatre. My seat was next to my old friend Stanley Beckwith, the timpanist. Just before the entry of the Meistersingers' March in the overture, he leant over to me and whispered in my ear, 'My sisters are giving me some new winter underwear for my birthday. Mine is full of holes.' A split second later his cue came and he unleashed a terrific cannonade, 'Pom pom pom pom . . . pom pom pom pom . . . pom pom pom pom'. A miraculous piece of timing!"

Needless to say, characterisation has to be sustained on an exit, until the actor is right off stage and out of view. Occasionally one sees a 'slump', a loss of concentration during the last few steps of an exit.

## When Do I and When Don't I Move?

Economy of movement should be aimed at. Restless, ineffective movements weaken a performance, unless used deliberately to show a trait in a particular character. Lomov, for example, in Chekov's *The Proposal* might well use a wealth of small, nervous hand movements to show that he is a hypochondriac. When an actor is listening to someone he should be still, except for necessary reactions. Movement of any kind on his own lines has to be carefully selected. A famous director used to tie cotton round the arms of his students then ask them to act out a speech. When their feeling was strong enough for them to break the cotton thread by a movement, that was the point at which gesture was subsequently incorporated into the performance. A vigorous movement after a period of stillness has the same effect as a shout after silence.

Movement in comedy and farce has to be judged very carefully. A sudden movement on a line which is designed to get a laugh will kill it stone dead, whether it is the actor who is speaking the line who moves, or someone else in the scene. Jealous actors have been known to kill fellow actors' comedy lines by this method.

It is difficult to stand still and to look natural on the stage when you have nothing to say or do for a long period. But if you appear to be interested in what is going on, are relaxed and do not fidget, you will not draw attention to yourself but become part of the scene. Repose is a valuable asset.

## How Do I Move?

Many factors affect they way in which a character moves: costume, climate, the age of the person represented. Not only his actual years but, even more important, whether he or she has 'worn well', or is prematurely aged, has to be borne in mind. Every available clue has to be picked up from the text - both from what the character says and from what others say about him. Questions such as has she had a sleepless night? is he suffering from jet-lag, or a hangover? have to be asked. Is the character convalescent? More realism is demanded from actors when they are supposed to be dying from tuberculosis in a play, than from opera singers supposed to be suffering from the same condition. The latter appear to retain the use of powerful lungs, right up to the bitter end.

States of mind obviously affect movement. Nervous agitation and stress may be revealed in hand movements. The use of the hands in acting makes an interesting study. I have seen an actor display passionate emotion with his voice and one hand, the other being completely relaxed.

Pace in movement reflects character, motivation and mood. Sometimes aimless, almost zombie-like moves are allowed to devitalise a performance. Controlled energy is always interesting to watch. It suggests that the actor has more power than he is actually using. Then, when he does unleash his full power it can be tremendously exciting. Robert Lindsay's performance as

Cyrano de Bergerac was a wonderful example of the use of controlled energy.

Basic technique in stage-movement is just the beginning. When an actor has mastered it he can go on to explore all the possibilities of visual expression. I have only touched on the subject of movement in period plays. Whole books have been devoted to this study and may be found in libraries. Once a young actor realises that movement and speech are both natural forms of expression and that he should not separate them in his mind when he is studying a part, many difficulties in suiting "the action to the word, the word to the action" will disappear.

# Chapter Five

# Improvisation

"Things are not important . . .
But . . . if everything around me on stage were true . . ."
*Stanislavski*

## Introduction

Improvisation has now become an umbrella-word and is used to cover all kinds of disparate activities. It has attracted fanatical discipleship on the one hand and obsessive suspicion on the other. It is best regarded as a tool, of great value when it is properly used and one capable of inflicting damage when it is not. Much has been said and written about its merits and demerits.

Its own supporters have done improvisation a disservice by claiming too much for its efficacy - in training actors, for example, and too much time has been devoted to it in drama classes in schools, to the exclusion of work on developing clear expressive speech and familiarising pupils with the work of first-rate, exciting writers.

In the theatre, its detractors have maintained a blinkered attitude to the way it can be used to explore characters and themes in rehearsal and to freshen actors during a long run. In the world of theatre-in-education, its critics have underestimated its powers of developing a child's imagination and ability to express itself.

It is a provocative subject which has aroused passionate feelings both for and against its use. Today it is being employed increasingly in areas outside the theatre and schools, sometimes by practitioners who do not understand what it can, and cannot, do. It has been confused with rôle-playing on courses for business and professional people, for example.

Within the theatre it has been regarded as the answer to all the problems an actor faces in the interpretation of a character. It has been thought of as the only subject of value in the speech and drama lesson in schools. It has been confused with mime and with Method acting. Some of its practitioners have taken Stanislavski's ideas about training an actor and misapplied them. In this connection, Jean Benedetti has written a book, *Stanislavski: An Introduction,* which clears up many of the misunderstandings about Stanislavski's System.

## Some Specific Uses of Improvisation

*Improvisation in Schools*

Here the primary aims are to release a child from inhibitions, to develop its imagination and powers of self-expression and to give it confidence. If properly handled, improvisation can inculcate a sense of responsibility to the group and encourage self-discipline. It can help a child to understand its own nature and encourage it to understand the other person's point of view.

*Improvisation in Drama Schools*

Here the objectives include helping the drama student to understand himself, his strengths and weaknesses; to overcome mental and emotional blocks; to encourage him to explore and extend his developing talents; and to increase his powers of physical and vocal expression and ability to express himself fluently. Group improvisations are useful as a preparation for ensemble acting.

*Improvisation in Rehearsals for Professional Productions*

The director will often use improvisation to help an actor to explore a text in depth in order to understand the character and situation in which he will be involved. The underlying themes in the play will be brought out in workshop sessions.

*Improvisation During the Long Run of a Play*

Sometimes during a long run an actor will become stale and mechanical. Improvisation sessions can be useful in giving him a new perspective on his rôle and fresh stimulus to his imagination.

## Improvisation in Theatre-in-Education

The way in which improvisation swept through school drama-teaching some years back was astonishing. I only realised to what extent it was used, when I was on a panel interviewing candidates for a three-year course designed to train specialist teachers of Speech and Drama. Over several years a series of applicants were asked "What do you consider to be the main value to a child of the speech and drama lesson?" Nine out of ten answered promptly "Improvisation." The interview continued along these lines, with these general reactions: "Would you cover anything else in these lessons?" - a puzzled silence; "What about speech?" - a reluctant perhaps; "Literature? Plays and poetry in particular?" - a blank expression; "Shakespeare?" - a look of ill-disguised distaste. It appeared that in the minds of the majority of those we interviewed 'improvisation' was synonymous with 'drama' and that it had been the main, if not the only, subject covered in their school drama lessons.

It also emerged that, in nearly all their experience, improvisation had been divorced from texts. However, one girl told us how she had been given improvisation exercises based on her set books at 'O' and 'A' level and that these had been of enormous help to her and had enabled her to achieve high grades. More recently, drama teachers have become much more aware of how improvisation exercises may be used to help their pupils to study set books and, particularly, Shakespeare's plays.

I have always wanted to try out the following improvisation with a class who were studying *Macbeth* for an examination. The broad outlines of the storyline and location would be given them, as in the *Commedia dell' Arte*. They would be asked to improvise the dialogue.

The setting is a household in the green-belt in the home counties. We have a gifted, but rather weak husband, who works for a large firm in the city. The Managing Director is overdue for retirement, but shows no signs of going. Until he does, the husband (who we will call Mr. MacIntosh) is kept in a subordinate position. Mrs MacIntosh is intensely ambitious for her husband and ready to go to any lengths to further his career. Both husband and wife are showing signs of strain. Unexpectedly, Sir Rex Daniels, the Managing Director, invites himself to the MacIntosh home and begs a bed for the night as he has a local engagement early the next morning. The situation unwinds, the murder has to be devised. The problems of Sir Rex's heir and the heir's son has to be solved. Both are already on the Board of Directors.

Alternative schemes for the disposal of these three obstacles to MacIntosh's career could be tried out. Mrs MacIntosh (and possibly the teacher in charge of the class) ends up on the psychiatrist's couch and reveals the crime under hypnosis.

I feel sure that the play would be very well known by the time that this exercise was finished, so long as fidelity to the spirit and meaning of Shakespeare's play was preserved and the approach did not become gimmicky. There should be no wilful working against the text.

Too often improvisation is treated as an easy option. The children are given a title or a sentence and left to work out a scene which they then act out. No constructive comment is given afterwards. The same thing happens at the next week's lesson and the next. No wonder the class gets bored with this aimless repetition.

It is a demanding subject for the teacher. It is difficult to provide exactly the right stimuli for each class and to know just how much is needed to trigger off an imaginative response. And then the lessons have to be structured in such a way that the children's imagination and capabilities are gradually stretched. Great concentration is needed whilst watching improvised scenes in order that helpful comments may be made at the end. Guidance has to be given without inhibiting the children. A teacher has to be constantly aware of the effects that this group activity is having on each child. Are the forceful, confident children swamping the creativity of the rest? Are they becoming self-indulgent as a group, or bored or lazy?

One cannot expect them to keep on producing fresh ideas in the same way as a conjurer produces coloured ribbons out of a hat, in a seemingly never-ending stream. The time will come when they will reach the end of their resources. Fresh knowledge, new experiences and stimuli have to be fed in.

A common danger is that children, and not only children, sometimes think that the aim of improvisation is not to be truthful, but to entertain, to make the rest of the group laugh. The class degenerates into a series of ego-trips; nothing is taken seriously. Much valuable lesson time may be wasted in this way. Showing-off has nothing to do with the true purpose of improvisation.

On the positive side, when the true purpose is understood and when the classes are carefully structured, particularly in the early stages, improvisation can be a valuable part of a drama lesson. It is especially useful in creating group feeling in today's multi-racial classes.

Improvised scenes can become the basis of a scripted play. I have seen dramatically effective material resulting from it. Nearly always, the children had been encouraged to be self-critical by their drama teacher and so banal, cliché-ridden dialogue and situations had been avoided. To paraphrase the writer, Ernest Hemingway, "If it acts easy, that's because it was improvised hard."

## Improvisation in Actor Training

This usually starts at the audition. A group is assembled, sometimes numbers are pinned on them, and they are given the stimulus of a subject - sunshine; a situation - a late-night party; or asked to imagine that the walls are icy-cold and they have to touch them. A girl may be told to make love to a chair. Reactions vary from embarrassment to brash confidence. Occasionally, there will be a truthful response. Some of the group will have had experience of improvisation at school, some will have had none at all.

Those accepted by a drama school will find that improvisation forms an important part of their training, particularly in their first year. The purposes of these improvisation classes vary considerably from school to school.

The intention may be to 'break down' a student. This is all very well, so long as he is able to put himself together again. I know of several students who were unable to do this. A pity, because some of them had considerable potential. It was interesting to hear Alec Guinness talking about this process in a radio interview. He said that he had never felt the need to be broken down and built up again as an actor. However, some people, undoubtedly find it a helpful method.

I am a little suspicious of students who say that they find improvisation easy. This can indicate a lack of depth and sensitivity. And so I was rather surprised by the first two sentences in Viola Spolin's *Improvisation for the Theatre*: "Everyone can act. Everyone can improvise." In my experience, this is certainly not the case. Some people never could act, cannot act now and never will be able to act. Even if they can improvise that does not mean that they will be able to act. In fact, I have noticed that some students who shone in improvisation classes have often failed to do well in the theatre after leaving drama school. Whereas, others who were very bad at improvisation have turned out to be good actors.

Fortunately, there are some gifted tutors who use improvisation exercises with such perception of the needs of individual students that they succeed in freeing them from their inhibitions: getting rid of mental blocks; releasing their emotions; and increasing their awareness of themselves and the world around them. Classes under such guidance are, of course, great value in training. Students taught to realise the importance of truth of the imagination and of feeling, in situation and character, become observant, develop powers of concentration and, eventually, achieve self-discipline.

There are one or two dangers that have to be guarded against. One is that a stereotyped response to similar situations may emerge. Another is that a girl or boy may always choose to improvise around the same emotion or character. In the end, these stereotypes become a defence and the imagination ceases to develop. Strictly speaking, the term 'improvisation' should only be used to describe an immediate response to a given word, situation or other stimuli (such as music, a picture or a colour). If this response is repeated, it ceases to become true improvisation. But, as in the school drama class, repetition of the original response can be valuable, particularly if the first reaction has been superficial or false.

Improvisations may be built up from the simplest stimuli. Exploration of the five senses usually evokes a lively response. Students need to be discouraged from being content with the obvious, but encouraged to think around the subject. Then a more varied reaction to the sense of smell, for example, might be elicited. It is nearly always bad smells that are imagined, although the dictionary definition of the word includes a scent or perfume.

Some of the most useful exercises are those based on empathy, trying to imagine what it would be like to be in someone else's shoes: to ask oneself how would I feel if I were accused of murder or of running a child over on a busy crossing? The word 'if' is a crucial one and has to be employed in order to understand Stanislavski's Method. This was to ask an actor to imagine what he would feel like if he were an oak tree for example. The approach was not to imagine that he was an oak tree but - I am I, but if I were an old oak set in certain surrounding conditions, what would I do?

Nöel Coward had a wicked sense of humour. The story goes that once, when he was being taken round a studio where Method Acting was being practised he asked various students "What are you?" Having received the replies "I am a table", "I am a chair" he finally turned to an actor in the corner and asked "And what are you?" "Please Mr. Coward, I am a glass of milk." "Then curdle" said Coward, walking away.

Just as in rehearsal an actor may go through blood, toil, tears and sweat to bring his rôle to life, so improvisation should be a dredging up from the depths. That is not to say that it is always a painful experience. The purging of the emotions may bring relief and after a stimulating session a student may experience a sense of fulfilment and a release from tension.

Improvisation should not, however, be regarded as the panacea for all ills. While it may improve fluency in speech, it does little to improve voice-production unless the exercises are chosen very carefully indeed. This is for two reasons. Firstly, true improvisation is not concerned with communication to an audience, so habits of quiet, confidential speaking may be formed. A student may grow so used to under-projecting his voice that he finds it difficult to communicate with an audience during an actual performance. And secondly, he may become accustomed to using slack articulation. In my experience most drama students, when given a free choice of situation, tend to use a worse standard of voice and speech than they would normally.

This difficulty can be overcome if situations and characters are chosen with the aim of encouraging vocal projection and clarity - a court of law with a battle going on between Counsel for the Prosecution and Counsel for the Defence, for example. I have sometimes taken a group of students to the Old Bailey or to the Law Courts in the Strand to observe judges and barristers in action. An improvised trial scene is usually a rewarding exercise, even without this stimulus.

To ensure a flexible use of the voice, situations may be set up where characters have to communicate with each other at great distances, or against a distracting noise, such as the hum of factory machinery or the sound of rushing water. A few such exercises should be enough to break a group of the habit of using the same level of voice and type of speech at every session.

## Structuring

The structuring of a series of exercises needs to be carefully considered to ensure that the individual, changing needs of a group of students are met. It is probably best to work with small groups at first and to amalgamate them as time goes on and confidence grows. Self-revelation in front of a large group of one's peers can be paralysing and, in fact, counter-productive, as it drives one in on oneself, especially at the start of training.

## Improvisation and the Professional Actor

A great deal depends on the ability of the director. Peter Brook has done some inspired and inspirational work in this country and abroad and demonstrated the value of the imaginative use of improvisation. A less gifted director can waste a good deal of rehearsal time and end up with a company of bored and frustrated actors. Tyrone Guthrie was a master at keeping rehearsals stimulating and alive. Once, I remember, the company laboured away all morning to get some special effect that he wanted. When, finally, we got it right, "Splendid", he called delightedly from the stalls, "Now let's try it a different way." He had a relaxed approach with young actors, we felt we would try anything for him. But with established, experienced players he could be very tough, even ruthless. "No tricks" he said to one well-known leading actress. "I don't know what you mean, Tony," she bridled. But she did.

Although Guthrie used improvisation sessions brilliantly in rehearsal, he did not overrate its importance. He said that a person who lacked imagination should not enter the profession and that the practice of taking people to the exact location in which a play was set was unnecessary. They should be able to imagine it.

## Exploration of Character

One of the chief values of improvisation in rehearsal is as a means of exploring character. The entire background of a character from early childhood to the age he has reached when the play opens can be imaginatively recreated. It is, in fact, the Wordsworthian philosophy of "the child is father of the man."

It is useful, too, to improvise scenes around the events which are supposed to occur immediately before the play starts and events which are supposed to happen when there is a time lapse during the play. So often, a playwright sets Act Two "one month later" or "a year later." In the case of a writer like J. B. Priestley who juggles with time, this method is especially helpful. His *Time and the Conways* is a case in point. The period between the youth and middle age of the characters provides a fertile field for the development of character by improvisation.

Sometimes, the future history of the characters in a play can be acted out. When I was directing *As You Like It* with a young cast, we found a session in which we imagined the four married couples in the play ten years later on, very helpful. It transpired that Rosalind and Orlando were still in love (after all, it is a romantic play - one of Shakespeare's sunlit comedies). The marriage of Celia and Oliver had, predictably, after such an unlikely, hasty wooing, gone on the rocks. Phoebe and Silvius had gradually developed a satisfactory relationship, largely because of Silvius' unselfish devotion. As for Touchstone and Audrey, they had managed to refute Jacques' gloomy prediction,

"... thy loving voyage is but for two months victuall'd",

and were still together albeit in a cat and dog relationship. Improvisation based on the text is seldom a waste of time.

Once the preliminary exploration of situation and character is over and rehearsals on the text have begun, improvisation may still be of great help to the actors. Suppose an actress has difficulty in understanding the emotion felt by her character at a certain point in the play. She cannot get over this hurdle without help. A relevant situation which is close to her own experience might be acted out. Take as an illustration a character who loses an only child through sudden illness. The young woman playing the part has never had this experience but could be asked to imagine what she felt when something in childhood was suddenly taken from her: the loss of a pet, for example, and the accompanying distress could be remembered.

I like the story of the actor who was playing a character in a play about the French Revolution who was told that he was going to be guillotined the next morning. The actor simply could not envisage what it would feel like to be in this situation. The director said to him, "What is one of the worst things that you can imagine happening to you?" "To be told that I would have to plunge into a cold bath during arctic weather." "All right - think of having to immerse yourself in that icy water, when you are told about your death sentence." The actor did so. And every night at the performance, audiences were shaken by the expression of sheer horror which came over his face at that moment.

I remember that during rehearsals of a student production I directed of *Everyman*, the medieval mystery play, great difficulty was experienced by the actor playing the main part, because he could not imagine what it would be like to die. In this particular case, no amount of improvisation of relevant situations helped because his imagination was not strong enough.

I once directed *The Trial of Mary Dugan* and one of the witnesses, who was supposed to be a flighty little girl, had trouble at first, in getting the voice and movement of the character. As soon as she was asked to imagine that she was a miniature French poodle, the realisation of her character became much easier for her. This time, no improvisation exercise was needed, as she had a vivid imagination. Sometimes one image is enough to release the creative powers of a performer.

## Improvisation During a Long Run of a Play

It is not only John Osborne's Archie Rice who can grow tired of the whole business of entertaining,

"I'm dead behind these eyes. I'm dead, just like the whole inert, shoddy lot out there. It doesn't matter because I don't feel a thing, and neither do they. We're just as dead as each other."

Most actors, during a very long run, have felt something akin to this at some time or other. Improvisation sessions are invaluable in freshening the imagination when players are becoming stale and mechanical in their performances.

Rôles may be switched, or the play may be placed in a different period. A fresh stimulus such as asking the cast to imagine and act out a different ending is sometimes found to be helpful.

The danger of growing stale is greater in a serious play than in a comedy or farce because, in the latter genres, audience reaction is more evident. Laughs have to be timed. No two audiences react to comedy and farce in quite the same way, so that each performance presents a fresh challenge. An actor is given warning that his performance is going off the boil if he suddenly finds that he is not getting a laugh in the customary place. Then he has to ask himself why?

It may be a question of timing, or it may be that he is becoming mechanical and not delivering the line freshly. This is more likely to happen at matinees with a thin house, when he is getting less stimulus from the audience, than at evening performances.

In comedy an actor is constantly being kept on his toes. In tragedy he may find, after a time, that his emotion is becoming externalised. In both these situations the revitalising power of improvisation may be used in workshop sessions.

## Coping with Emergencies

There is no doubt that improvisation exercises sharpen the wits. Being able to deal with unexpected situations is an asset. One of the most common emergencies which may arise during a performance is when an actor forgets his lines or 'dries'. There are numerous stories, both true and apocryphal, about how people have coped with this situation.

Actors playing in Shakespeare sometimes develop the facility of improvising a line of verse when they 'dry' - and even making it scan. Kenneth Branagh described, in his autobiography *Beginning*, how he improvised several lines of blank verse when an essential property was missing from the stage in a scene from *Henry V* at Stratford.

The resourceful are able to improvise whole speeches when they have forgotten the author's lines. This happens most frequently on first nights in a repertory company when rehearsal time has been short.

Quick wits can rescue a plot from disaster as, for example, when someone who has two rather similar speeches, one in Act One and one in Act Three, suddenly plunges into the later one half way through the first act. Hasty rewriting of the playwright's dialogue is needed. It is more difficult when the play is a whodunnit and the vital clue has been prematurely given away.

Another emergency which has to be dealt with is when an actor is late for his entrance - is 'off'. Before improvisation was used so extensively in an actor's training, rather lame dialogue used to be invented to cover this wait - "I think I hear him coming", "he must be arriving at any minute." Now actors may get so carried away by their own powers of invention that they are almost disappointed when the missing character appears.

Sometimes players have to cover-up mistakes made by the stage-management. Of these, missing props are among the most common. I was once the Assistant Stage Manager in a company and suddenly realised, when the curtain went up on the second act, that I had forgotten to put the telephone on. Douglas Byng, who was playing the butler was supposed to answer it. I stood in the wings, tense with anxiety. When the cue came, I desperately pressed the telephone bell button off stage. Whereupon he calmly said to the lady of the house, "Excuse me madam, I think I hear the telephone ringing on the extension in the bathroom", proceeded to walk off, pick up the telephone, carry it on and fix it into an imaginary plug under the table. He swept away my embarrassed apology afterwards, as if it were a matter of no account: a kindly man.

## Some Disadvantages

The advantages of improvisation should be weighed against the disadvantages. Directors, drama tutors and teachers who understand what it can and cannot do are in the minority.

By far the most insidious danger which may arise from the overuse of improvisation is the development in a group of actors of a lack of consideration for the audience, for the customer. This attitude is more common than one would imagine, in both the professional and amateur theatre. I have heard amateur directors say, "The audience will hate our next play, we are doing it for ourselves." All well and good, but in that case, why bother to have an audience and, what is more, why ask them to pay for being bored stiff?

Overuse of improvisation during the rehearsal period can delay work on the text for so long that the actual performance suffers. A habit of vocal under-projection and slack articulation could be formed. This might be appropriate for the majority of exercises used, but will be a disadvantage to the performer when he has to communicate with an audience.

Too much discussion before getting onto the text may actually stultify the imagination. One of the actor's most priceless possessions, an instinctive response to words, may be lost.

A young actor friend of mine told me of a rehearsal in which,

"we all sat around and discussed the play, then we did an improvisation based on the theme and then we got onto the actual text. The result was awful. The most voluble in the discussion seemed to be the worst at bringing the words to life."

When I was adjudicating at the finals of the National Union of Students' Drama Festival, sponsored by *The Sunday Times*, a worrying trend was noticeable, time and time again. In discussions about their productions after the finals, the student directors spoke confidently, and even brilliantly, about the plays and their intentions behind their direction of them. However, what the audience had actually witnessed the night before bore little resemblance to what the director and cast now declared had been their aims in producing the play.

Improvisation may result in driving an actor in on himself so that, eventually, not only is he unable to connect with an audience but also unable to make contact with the rest of the cast. In a play by Chekov, for instance, this would be a disastrous state of affairs.

Just occasionally, a good play will emerge from group improvisation, as did *Abigail's Party*. Mike Leigh was successful in combining different elements into a cohesive whole. More often, in less experienced hands, the experiment results in a shapeless, self-indulgent and overlong piece of work, a mixture of warring styles.

## 'Method' Acting

Rod Steiger described in an interview, the splendid early days of The Actors' Studio and the 'Method' and how, later on, it grew too large, observers were allowed in and some of the earlier inspiration was lost. He thought that the improvisation exercises were becoming an end in themselves and that their true objective was being lost. Certainly, some later exponents of the 'Method' have been notorious for their failure to make themselves heard and understood.

## Some Conclusions

Ultimately, the value of improvisation to the actor depends on the way the director handles it. It should be structured and progressive. It should not be expected to do more than it is capable of doing. It should be regarded as a potentially useful tool.

We must continue to value the contribution that the proper use of improvisation can bring to drama in schools, in further education, in actor training and in both the professional and amateur theatre. But the audience must not be forgotten. We would all do well to bear in mind Dr. Samuel Johnson's words,

> "The drama's laws, the drama's patrons give,
> For we that live to please, must please to live."

# Chapter Six

# Playing in Shakespeare

"Oh it takes a lifetime to grow up to Shakespeare."
*T. S. Eliot at seventy.*

At some time in his career an actor may be faced with the challenge of a part in Shakespeare, the greatest master of language in our dramatic literature. If so, he will also be faced with the weight of tradition which lies on the most frequently performed of the plays. Consider the traditions made by the succession of actors who have played Hamlet, for instance. Burbage was followed by Joseph Taylor. Burbage rehearsed him in the part. Taylor's performance was seen by Sir William Davenant who taught Betterton the role. When Garrick was playing Hamlet he was able to find out from the old actors of Betterton's company what stage business Betterton had used. Edmund Kean, in his turn, learned from the old actors who had worked with Garrick. In the late nineteenth and early twentieth centuries Henry Irving heard from Chippendale, who had play-ed Polonius to Kean's Hamlet, what that great actor had done with the part. Ellen Terry, who had played Ophelia to Irving's Hamlet, was the aunt of John Gielgud whose performance of the part is a legend in his lifetime.

Some Hamlets have incorporated what they felt was valu-able from past performances; some have brought to the part new insights; some have gone to extremes in their desire to do something different and have given an interpretation which was idiosyncratic and even perverse. Shakespeare's character has been lost in performances built on gimmickry. No-one wishes Shakespeare's plays and characters to be sacrosanct, preserved in the amber of time but, in their determination to make his plays relevant to today, some directors have inflicted great damage on them - sacrificing dramatic impact and losing the indefinable mystery of the genius which created them.

Today's directors have often, it is true, succeeded in scra-ping off some of the false accretions of time. Sometimes an inspired director is able to bring fresh life and vigour to a familiar play. But it seems strange that so often nowadays our greatest playwright seems to be prized for everything except his language.

I am always interested to hear the opinions of young play-goers who come fresh to Shakespeare. I have found that these are the ones who are most critical of gimmicky productions which work against the text and the spirit and meaning of the play.

In her book, *In Defence of the Imagination*, Helen Gardner gives her views about Shakespeare in the director's theatre:

"Often the plays are radically cut, scenes added and business introduced in flat contradiction with words being spoken, or with the import of a scene, to make the play accord with certain critical interpretations."

In an amusing talk, Donald Sinden once described how we have progressed from an actor's theatre, to an actor-manager's theatre, to a director's theatre and are now in the age of the sponsor's theatre - the sponsor being given equal or even larger billing than the name of the play, the author, the leading actor or the director. I have a suspicion that Shakespeare, being a businessman, might not have objected to this latest turn of events.

## Speaking the Verse

We live in a prosaic age. This is shown in our lifestyle, in our attitude to the arts in general and, in particular, in our mistrust of poetry. In the theatre this attitude is most strikingly demonstrated by the way actors approach the speaking of blank verse.

### Blank Verse

What is blank verse? There is no mystique about it. It is simply unrhymed verse, generally consisting of ten syllables in a line, divided into five feet, each containing two syllables - one stressed and one unstressed. Some writers use a form of blank verse consisting of four feet and eight syllables. A foot in this metre is described as an *iamb* and Shakespeare's plays are, for the most part written in five foot iambic lines: these are sometimes referred to as *decasyllabic* lines. Breaking the line up into feet and noting any irregularities is called *scansion*.

### The Iambic Metre

The iambic metre is the nearest of the four main metres in English to natural speech. And because of its structural resemblance to ordinary speech, speakers with no previous knowledge of blank verse or of scansion are sometimes able to speak Shakespeare very well indeed. Students and actors can take the *iambic pentameter* in their stride, if they have a good ear.

Nevertheless, I believe that a knowledge of scansion is of great value to an actor whether he has a good ear or not. Unfortunately this knowledge is rare. When we understand the way that Shakespeare used irregularities, we gain an insight into how he intended the lines to be spoken. Thus the meaning is illuminated and we have a better perception of the character.

*Scansion*

There is an underlying beat of unstressed and stressed syllables in Shakespeare's lines. But he does not always conform to the strict pattern of the iambic pentameter.

$$u— / u — / —u / u —/ u —/$$

He uses irregularities. When these are understood, they are of enormous value as they enable the actor to speak the lines with apparent spontaneity and naturalness, as if they have been freshly thought.

*Irregularities*

One of the most important irregularities to study is the use of *inversion*. That is the substitution of a *trochaic foot* (a stressed syllable followed by an unstressed one) for an iambic. This gives the speaker a clue as to where the emphasis should be placed.

Here are a few examples:

"but I do think it is their husband's faults
If wives do fall. *Say* that they slack their duties.'

"What raging of the sea, *shaking* of earth."

These are examples of the *trochaic inversion* within the line. Far more common is the inversion at the beginning of a line, in the first foot. Over and over again, Shakespeare uses it to give additional impetus and strength to the word, as in the following:

"When you shall these unlucky deeds relate,
*Speak* of me as I am."

"*Sleep* that knits up the ravell'd sleave of care."

"Will all great Neptune's ocean wash this blood
*Clean* from my hand?"

"Eternity was in our lips and eyes,
*Bliss* in our brows bent,"

"The barge she sat in, like a burnish'd throne,
*Burned* on the water."

If, however, the shape of the verse is not preserved, and the lines are run into each other whenever the sense runs through from one line to the next, the force of the stressed word at the beginning of the second line of the *enjambment* is lost. A fractional pause should be made at the end of the first line and no breath should be taken.

## Use of the Pyrrhic and Spondee

Sometimes Shakespeare puts two unstressed syllables in a foot - a pyrrhic. It is essential that this is recognised and that the speaker does not turn it into an iamb, in the mistaken belief that it is necessary to bring out a regular metrical beat. This irregularity gives fluency and naturalness to the line and if it is ignored the players reduce Shakespeare's flexible rhythms to the insistent 'dum dee dum' of classroom repetition. It is this kind of speaking which puts school children off Shakespeare.

Here is an example of a *pyrrhic foot*:

"Or thou, / the great / est sol / *dier of* / the world."

This is an obvious one, but the speaker has to be on his guard to pick up the less obvious occurrences of the irregularity.

Shakespeare sometimes uses two stressed syllables in a foot - a *spondee*. Deciding when he intends a foot to be spoken with two stresses raises interesting points of interpretation. Take the following familiar line:

"The quality of mercy is not strain'd"

Should it be "not strained" (a spondee) or "not strain'd" (an iamb) or even "not strain'd" (a trochee). I favour the second of these readings, but there is a case to be made out for each of them.

## The Feminine Ending

Shakespeare tends to use an extra, unstressed syllable at the end of a line more frequently as his style develops. This irregularity, if it is recognised, is of value to the actor as it gives a sense of ease and fluency, for example:

90

> "Life's but a walking shadow, a poor player,
> That struts and frets his hour upon the stage,
> And then is heard no more; it is a tale
> Told by an idiot, full of sound and fury,
> Signifying nothing."

Here the first and fourth lines have *feminine endings*. However, if the lines are all run together (a current fashion) the extra syllables of "player" and "fury" will lose their value and the rhythm of the speech will be lost.

## Counterpoint

When blank verse is well spoken, one of the interests to the ear is the way that the *iambic stress* usually falls on the natural speech stress, but sometimes does not so that one is aware of a basic beat underneath and also of a kind of counterpoint on top, when the two kinds of stress fail to coincide.

## Pause

Bound up with scansion is the use of pause. The neglect of the *suspensive pause*, that is the slight pause at the end of a line when the sense runs on into the following one, will ruin some of Shakespeare's finest passages. Take, for instance, Perdita's lines from *The Winter's Tale*:

> " . . . daffodils,
> That come before the swallow dares, and take
> The winds of March with beauty."

Usually one hears,

> "daffodils that come before the swallow dares and take the winds of March with beauty,"

or, more rarely

> " . . . daffodils
> That come before the swallow dares and take *(long pause and
>                                                 intake of breath)*
> The winds of March with beauty."

In both of these examples the heart-stopping effect of the word "take" at the end of the line, giving the actor the chance to linger almost imperceptibly on it, is lost. It is the slight weighting of the word which gives it poignancy.

The *caesural pause*, a natural break in a line of blank verse, occasionally marked by punctuation, gives a rhythmic, balancing effect. It is less often ignored by the speaker, because it enables him to take a breath. Its proper use gives significance to the words, especially when it follows a key word. Its varied position in the line breaks the regular tramp of the *iambic feet*. Think of soldiers marching across a bridge being asked to break step, to avoid strain on the structure. Think of the effect of a too steady *iambic beat* on the ears of the audience.

Shakespeare varied its position more frequently in his later plays than in his earlier ones. Here is an example of the varied position of the caesural pause:

> "O sun
> Burn the great sphere than mov'st in // Darkling stand
> The varying shore o' th' world // O Antony,
> I faint. // O Iras, Charmian! 'Tis no matter.
> Go to the fellow, good Alexis; // bid him
> Report the feature of Octavia, her years,
> Her inclination; // let him not leave out
> The colour of her hair."

Shakespeare has thus given clear indications in his speeches as to when an actor should take a breath. Sir John Gielgud has said

"If you give yourself to a Shakespeare speech and really look at the punctuation, the breath pauses nearly always come in the right places."

The actor can, of course, take a breath at the end of an end-stopped line, when the sense ends at the end of the line, without upsetting the rhythm, but he should not in a suspensive pause. There is much more, naturally, to the playing of Shakespeare than speaking his blank verse well. But actors who let Shakespeare's language 'carry' them, will find their task of creating a character much easier than those who fight against the construction of the verse.

## Pointing the Lines

One of the chief criticisms made against actors in general today is that they cannot be heard in parts of the auditorium. These complaints cannot be written off as coming exclusively from the elderly and the hard of hearing, because they are voiced by students and schoolchildren as well. I believe that the reasons for this failure on the part of the actors comes from four basic causes.

The most obvious of these is poor voice production and weak articulation. The second is insufficient motivation to communicate with an audience. The third is an inability to adjust vocal projection when a production moves from a small theatre to one with a large auditorium. The fourth is that the actor is not 'pointing' the lines sufficiently - that is he is not picking out the key or operative words and making them stand out from the rest. It is particularly important to point a speech when one is playing in Shakespeare, because the language is often difficult and obscure. When the lines are pointed the audience will get the drift of what the character is saying and even if they fail to understand a word or two, the outline of the speech will emerge.

When I was a student, I went to Paris to stay for a few days in some theatrical lodgings. My first view of the city was at night from a road on the outskirts. Paris was blazing with light and looked like a necklace of diamonds on a black velvet cloth. I could see the outline of the necklace, the bigger stones, but I could not see the connecting links of smaller stones as clearly, however, I could imagine them. A carefully pointed speech is like that. When the key words stand out, the audience is made aware of the outline of the development of the character's thoughts. Pointing is achieved by the selective use of emphasis - selective is the key word here. If too many words in a sentence are emphasised it will be as bad as if none are. The effect on the audience will be that they gradually lose interest because the strain of concentrating on an over-forceful delivery will become too great. Many actors playing in Shakespeare today fall into this trap: there is a tendency to hammer out the lines.

## Shakespeare's Use of Antithesis

Shakespeare used rhetorical devices in both his blank verse and his prose. One of the most frequently used is antithesis, a contrast of ideas. Sometimes this is easy to recognize and to bring out, but sometimes the antitheses have to be teased out of the text. These may range from two opposed ideas, to three or even four. There are many examples of simple antithesis. For instance, when Falstaff says,

> "I have more flesh than another man,
> and therefore more frailty"

it is obvious that the key words are "flesh" and "frailty". Sometimes the contrast is condensed into a phrase as when Queen Margaret says of King Henry,

> "His study in his tilt-yard."

A slightly less obvious use occurs in *King John,*

> "How oft the sight of means to *do* ill deeds
> Makes deeds ill *done.*"

Examples of *double antithesis* abound. Shakespeare ends the sonnet *When Forty Winters Shall Besiege Thy Brow* with the line,

> "And see thy blood warm when thou feel'st it cold."

The speaker needs to set the word "see" against "feel" and "warm" against "cold". This is chiefly an imaginative process. He has to avoid too obvious a use of emphasis, which would give an explanatory effect, but try to picture in his mind what is being described.

In *Richard II* there is a whole sequence of double antitheses. Here he is talking to Bolingbroke from the walls of Flint Castle. He starts with a simple juxtaposition of ideas,

> "I'll give my jewels for a set of beads"

and then the thoughts are elaborated,

> "My gay apparel for an almsman's gown,
> My figur'd goblets for a dish of wood . . .
> And my large kingdom for a little grave."

94

These lines, spoken by Queen Margaret in *Henry VI*, need particular care as they contain the triple use of antithesis,

"Small curs are not regarded when they grin
But great men tremble when the lion roars."

"Small curs" are opposed to "lion", "grin" is opposed to "roars" and "not regarded" to "tremble".

Once the contrasted ideas have been recognized by the actor, he has to decide how to bring them out without sounding didactic or explanatory. He will find that inflection is a much more subtle means of emphasis than added stress. An useful method is to employ a rising inflection for the first idea and a compound one, that is a combination of a falling and rising glide of the voice, for the second.

"Let us be sacrificers, but not butchers".

## Added Stress

Sometimes added stress may be used as a means of emphasis with great effect as, for example in *Richard II*,

**Northumberland:**
. . . may it please you to come down?

**King Richard:**
*Down, down* I come, like glist'ring Phaethon.

and in *King Henry IV*,

**Hotspur:**
. . . for he made me *mad*
To see him shine so brisk.

Some actors tend to use added stress as their main, or even sole, means of emphasis.

## Intensity

This has already been referred to in the chapter on modulation. It is a highly effective method of pointing words, if used with discretion. I shall never forget how Richard Burton, as Henry V, in the speech before Agincourt spoke the line,

"We *few*, we *happy* few, we band of brothers."

He spoke it very quietly on a fairly high pitch but with such emotional pressure behind the words, that the effect on the audience was stunning.

Laurence Olivier demonstrated, in two striking examples, the power of intensity in pointing a whole line in his film version of *Henry V*. The first is in Act I, Scene 2. The Dauphin has sent his ambassador to the English Court with a gift, accompanied by this message,

**First Ambassador:**

. . . The Prince our master
Says that you savour too much of your youth,
And bids you be advis'd there's nought in France
That can be with a nimble galliard won;
You cannot revel into dukedoms there.
He therefore sends you, meeter for your spirit,
This tun of treasure . . .

**King Henry:**

What treasure, uncle?

**Exeter:**

Tennis-balls, my liege.

Then follows a pause in which we see the King's face in close-up. He narrows his eyes and replies with a deadly, chilling intensity,

"We are glad the Dauphin is so pleasant with us."

Here every word is made to work.

The second example is in the fourth act . We have seen the French quitting the battlefield after riding through the English camp where they slaughtered the boys who have been left with the army's baggage. The King is shown the body of one of these young victims. There is a pause, then he says, again very quietly but with deep emotion,

"I was not angry since I came to France."

96

Such is the power of intensity in pointing a line that these two moments stand out in a play which is full of declamatory speeches.

## The Use of Pause

This method of pointing a line of blank verse needs to be handled with discretion. If the pause is over-long, or used too often, the rhythm and flow of the verse will be lost. Some actors, striving for originality make an eccentric use of pause and lose the meaning of the line. On the other hand, an actor bringing a fresh approach to a well-known speech can, by deliberately breaking the usual pattern, isolate a word and give it new dramatic significance. Ian McKellen did this in the "Tomorrow, and tomorrow, and tomorrow" speech in *Macbeth*.

At the end of Richard II's great speech, "No matter where - of comfort no man speak" there is an opportunity for an actor to point a line effectively by means of pause,

"I live with bread like you, feel want,
Taste grief, // need friends."

## Handling Repetition

One of the most useful things that I learned from a fellow-actor was how to handle repetition when the same word recurs at short intervals in a speech. To avoid 'hammering' it after the first mention, he said that you have to search for the accompanying qualifying word at every subsequent repetition.

This technique is so often neglected, that it is worth giving two extended illustrations of its use. Both are drawn from modern plays. The first is from *Fear and Misery in the Third Reich* (the title is variously translated) by Bertolt Brecht:

**The Jewish Wife:**

It's a question of *time. Character* is a question of time. It lasts for a certain *length* of time, just like a glove. There are good ones that last a *long* time. But they don't last for ever.

The second is from Tennessee Williams' *The Glass Menagerie*,
**Amanda:**

> So lovely, that country in May. All lacy with dogwood, literally
> flooded with *jonquils*. That was the spring I had the *craze* for
> jonquils. Jonquils became an absolute *obsession*. Mother said,
> 'Honey, there's no more *room* for jonquils.' And still I kept on
> bringing in *more* jonquils . . . I made the young men help me
> *gather* the jonquils.

In both these examples, varied ways of bringing out the qualifying words should be used.

So far we have been considering the approach to speaking
blank verse. Many of the techniques already described also
apply to Shakespeare's prose.

## The Approach to Shakespeare's Prose

Shakespeare's use of prose develops from the earthy dialogue of lowlife characters in some of his early plays to the
sophisticated repartee of his middle period and finally to the
charged emotional speeches of a Hamlet or King Lear, in the
period of the tragedies. Each of these styles of writing calls for
a corresponding style of vocal expression. But they have one
thing in common, they are all rhythmical.

Launce in *The Two Gentlemen of Verona* has a long speech
about his dog Crab. This should not be difficult for the actor
because of the balance of the phrases and the way the speech
is structured so that the narrative carries the audience along to
the climax and to the comedy ending. In fact, Shakespeare does
most of the work for the actor if he will let him. Too often though,
Launce's speeches are smothered by an exaggerated clownish
accent and by superimposed comedy business - which distract
attention from the words (this may be why RADA has included
one of them in a list of speeches not to be performed at their
auditions). The 'Crab' speech does need, however, more than a
response to Shakespeare's rhythms. The voice has to be coloured in subtly different ways according to whether Launce is
addressing the audience in general, his dog, or giving his idea

of the voices of the Duke, three different lords and "the fellow who whips the dogs." In fact, taken out of context, the speech makes a splendid exercise in the use of varied tone colour.

Grumio in Act Four of *The Taming of the Shrew* has two short speeches in which he tells Curtis, Petruchio's other servant, to prepare for his master's arrival with Katherina and describes the horrors of their journey through mire in the freezing cold. Both speeches have rhythms which are helpful to the actor but both are technically difficult to bring off successfully as they depend on sustained attack and a vivid imagination.

In his middle period, Shakespeare showed great versatility in his use of prose. The style in *As You Like It* ranges from the wit of the court characters, Rosalind, Celia and Touchstone, to the rustic observations of Corin and Audrey.

The play begins with Orlando's resentment of his treatment by his brother. A recent Orlando has described how in rehearsal and in early performances he took it at breakneck speed, but later slowed it down. This I believe, was the right decision, as Orlando's first speech is an exposition of facts which are necessary for the audience to know. Also, an audience needs a few moments to get their ears attuned to an actor's voice, especially at the beginning of a play when they may not be completely settled in their seats.

Touchstone's lines are notoriously difficult to put across. This is partly because much of his comedy depends upon word play and some of the words he uses are now archaic. However, a resourceful comedy actor can get laughs from the way he handles the rhythms and times his lines, even though the audience cannot always understand what he is saying. Kenneth Branagh, in a Renaissance Company production, is one of the few actors I have seen play Touchstone who were able to make the lines amusing.

The mock wooing scene between Orlando and the disguised Rosalind is written entirely in prose. There are subtle mood changes which are reflected in the prose style as Rosalind veers between enjoyment of teasing her suitor:

"The poor world is almost six thousand years old, and in all this time there was not any man died in his own person, videlicet, in a love-cause,"

and the near sadness of her realisation that romantic love does not endure into marriage:

"Men are April when they woo, December when they wed."

The prose here becomes lyrical and the actress must be prepared to respond vocally to the shift in style.

In the great tragedies, Shakespeare's prose became a more powerful medium of dramatic expression. Instead of the flowing phrases, he uses a simpler, more economical style, making use of monosyllables. He never did this more strikingly than in *Hamlet*:

"What a piece of work is man! How noble in reason! How infinite in faculties! In form and moving, how express and admirable! In action, how like an angel! In apprehension how like a god! The beauty of the world! The paragon of animals! And yet, to me, what is this quintessence of dust?"

The speeches are charged with emotion, as when Hamlet accepts man's destiny,

"we defy augury: there is a special providence in the fall of a sparrow. If it be now, 'tis not to come; if it be not to come, it will be now; if it be not now, yet it will come - the readiness is all."

How can the actor best tackle these great speeches? The feeling has to be true, the voice generally quiet. A fairly measured pace will suggest philosophical thought; a subtle colouring of the tone will convey nuances of meaning. If the actor is wise he will keep still. The words have enough weight to make their effect without extraneous help from him.

## Four Great Performances

I have, in my playgoing life, seen four performances of Shakespearean rôles which were so unforgettable that I am still able to recreate them in my imagination as vividly as when I first saw them. The first of these experiences was Ralph Richardson's

Falstaff. I was there on the first night when he played it at the New Theatre. What was it about this performance that made it definitive? There was the appearance, of course. Even though bloated with sack, he carried himself with a grace that showed he had known better days. Then there was the voice - deep, resonant, with its rounded vowel sounds. Richardson was intensely loveable in the part. Even when he was lying, cheating, boasting, womanising, playing the coward, you loved the man. James Agate, the drama critic of *The Sunday Times* said of him that he "still keeps some of his fallen day about him." This added to the infectious enjoyment he brought to the part and made him a great Falstaff. I wrote in my diary that night that, "Richardson was Falstaff from his toe nails to the top of his head." I must have been thinking of what they told us at RADA - "act with your toe-nails."

Then there was John Gielgud's Hamlet at the Lyceum. Those who only know him from his film and television appearances in character parts in the nineteen seventies, eighties and nineties can have little idea of the extraordinary magnetism of his acting at this earlier period of his career.

It is fashionable now to criticize Gielgud as being overly musical in his delivery of blank verse. But his immaculate judgement of emphatic values and incisive use of consonants ensure that the sense of the words is never swamped by the sound. Among the great moments of his Hamlet was the first entrance. There was no doubt that this solitary figure was the Prince of Denmark. Gielgud had played the part three times before and was now completely immersed in the mood of bitter grief which was immediately established.

The moment I remember as being the most moving, however, was during his speech to Rosencrantz and Guildenstern in Act Two:

"I have of late, but wherefore I know not, lost all my mirth, forgone all custom of exercises; and indeed it goes so heavily with my disposition that this goodly frame, the earth, seems to me a sterile promontory; this most excellent canopy the air, look you, this brave o'erhanging firmament, this majestical roof fretted with golden fire - why,

it appeareth no other thing to me than a foul and pestilent congrega-
tion of vapours."

The depth of the actor's disillusionment matched the language.

Gielgud was especially fine too in the churchyard scene.
His ear for rhythm carried him triumphantly through the "Alas
poor Yorick!" speech with its nostalgia merging into grim humour,

"I knew him, Horatio: a fellow of infinite jest, of most excellent
fancy; he hath borne me on his back a thousand times ... where be your
gibes now, your gambols, your songs, your flashes of merriment that
were wont to set the table on a roar? Not one now to mock your own
grinning - quite chap-fall'n? Now get you to my lady's chamber, and
tell her, let her paint an inch thick, to this favour she must come."

It was while watching Donald Wolfit in the part of King
Lear that I first came to understand fully the meaning of the
word catharsis - a purging of the emotions. I have seen many
actors tackle this most demanding of parts, from Randle
Ayrton at Stratford to Olivier on stage and television. But Wolfit
was the only Lear who, in my opinion, managed to convey both
the power of the storm scenes and the tragic pathos of the last
act, with equal success. His production of *King Lear* was unre-
markable; the cast not worthy of him, but Wolfit overrode all
difficulties. The audience sat on hard seats, mesmerised. At the
end we stumbled out, feeling drained of emotion. During the
run of the play Wolfit kept asking the stage management to raise
the sound level of the thunder in the storm scenes. He could
make his voice heard over the loudest sound effects.

Some moments in the last act were almost unbearable in
their tragic power as, for instance, when he carried on the dead
Cordelia and mourned over her body,

"No, no, no life!
Why should a dog, a horse, a rat have life
And thou no breath at all? Thou'lt come no more,
Never, never, never, never never."

He was completely convincing in his mad scenes on the heath.
He mimed the stage business that accompanied,

> "Look, look a mouse!
> Peace, peace; this piece of toasted cheese will do't."

with great simplicity and utter absorption. That was a riveting moment in a towering performance which was full of them.

Olivier's Richard III was an extravagant creation. He had been worried about playing the part all through rehearsals and even up to the first night. However, he was able to capitalise on the particular gifts of his temperament to such an extent that it is not surprising that he made a tremendous success as Richard.

One of his most remarkable achievements was to make the wooing scene and the unlikely capitulation of the Lady Anne, always considered to be an almost insurmountable problem, completely credible. He exuded a glittering charm, insidiously sexual, which seemed to hypnotise her. One was reminded of a rabbit and a snake.

His mastery of the audience was established in his first speech, spoken softly with an underlying menace and a glint of black humour,

> "Now is the Winter of our discontent
> Made glorious summer by this sun of York; "

And there was quirky, self-parody in,

> "Grim-visag'd war hath smooth'd his wrinkled front,
> And now, instead of mounting barbed steeds
> To fright the souls of fearful adversaries,
> He capers nimbly in a lady's chamber
> To the lascivious pleasing of a lute."

This is the speech I remember best. What impressed me most about the whole performance was its authority and power over the audience. And it was controlled acting. All Olivier's gift for visual comedy was brought into play but he always related it to the text.

Of these four actors one could say, adapting Cassius' description of Julius Caesar, "Why, man they did bestride the narrow world like the Colossi." All found and conveyed the truth of their characters.

In all acting, Shakespearean or modern, surely it is truth that matters: truth of the imagination; truth of feeling; and truth

to the character as it is revealed in the words he speaks. The wise
actor realises this and trusts his playwright. And where does
technique come into it? Gielgud has answered this question
succinctly, in words which drive to the heart of the matter:

> "Truth is what we all strive for in acting. Yet acting can never be
> truth, it has to seem to be truthful, but carefully observed, selected and
> then conveyed to the audience in movement, costume, voice and
> action."

# Chapter Seven

# Playing in Comedy and Farce

"The best actors in the world, either for tragedy, comedy, history, pastoral, pastoral-comical, historical-pastoral, tragical-historical, tragical-comical, historical-pastoral."
*Polonius*

There are almost as many types of comedy as there are the types of plays described by Polonius: high comedy; black comedy; comedy of manners; kitchen comedy; burlesque. But whatever the genre there are factors which remain constant. Comedy comes from incongruity and surprise. It may arise out of the actual words spoken, for example: Oscar Wilde's epigrams; Neil Simon's one-liners; or from the listener's reaction to the line. Paul Eddington, in *Yes Minister* and *Yes Prime Minister*, was a master of this art. It may arise from the actor's sense of rhythm and timing, from situation or character.

105

In this chapter, I propose first to consider four different genres: *Restoration Comedy; Late Eighteenth Century Comedy; Wildean Comedy;* and the *Comedy of Nöel Coward.* I shall then turn to the consideration of farce.

## Restoration Comedy

The term Restoration Comedy is often loosely used to include the plays of Richard Sheridan and Oliver Goldsmith. However, these plays appeared a full forty years after the Restoration comedies of Congreve, Wycherley, Vanbrugh and Farquhar. A completely different style of acting is required for *She Stoops to Conquer* than for *The Way of the World.*

Restoration Comedy is popular at the moment and there are many revivals. But one seldom sees a production in which all the cast succeed in catching the appropriate style. It is, indeed, a most demanding one.

The first essential is for the actor to think himself back into the social climate of the period. I was going to say 'moral climate' but the Restoration period was amoral. The characters in the plays do not recognize a code of morality. The sexual innuendoes have to be delivered without any suggestion that the character finds them improper or daring. Charles II's lifestyle, and that of his courtiers, was in complete contrast to that of the Puritan Cromwell, and is reflected in the plays of the period.

What was the soil which fed the exotic, some would say 'un-English', bloom of Restoration Comedy? Its roots are both native and foreign. In the eighteen years preceding 1660 nearly all theatres in England were closed. Music, dancing, even the wearing of bright colours, were discouraged. It was a time of rigid morality. Charles had fled to Paris with his court and there they had seen the comedies of Molière in which the exaggerated manners of high society were satirised. And so, when they returned to England they brought with them new ideas which were grafted on to the native stock and a new spirit appeared in

106

the theatre. It was not only the style of writing that altered, but the theatres themselves had changed since Shakespeare's time.

Gone were the round or octagonal playhouses and instead a theatre oblong in shape had emerged from the adaptation of real tennis courts. Gone, too, was the close contact with the audience provided by the Elizabethan open, thrust stage. Now there was a proscenium arch, with a small apron.

In Restoration Comedy new styles of writing, a new attitude to sex, a new type of theatre combine. It is important for the modern actor in these plays to get the historical perspective right. And then real characters have to be created. We must believe in the characters in Restoration Comedy - it is only the plot that is difficult to believe in or, indeed, even to follow at times.

The modern actor has not only to cope with wearing the costume and handling the accessories correctly, but also with delivering the lines with point, clarity and apparently careless ease; and with enjoyment too. Congreve was an Irishman with all the Irish love of language. He has transmitted this love to his characters. They should relish their wit. Here is how Edmund Gosse, the literary critic, has summed up Congreve's style,

"Congreve balances, polishes, sharpens his sentences till they seem like a set of instruments prepared for an electrical experiment; the current is his unequalled wit."

A great deal is required of the actor vocally: a flexible voice; firm, but not overdone, articulation, even when speaking very rapidly. He needs to be able to use inflection well and to speak long phrases on one breath. He needs a good ear for the rhythm and balance of the lines. And he must speak like a human being; too often an unreal, unnatural voice and exaggerated inflections are adopted.

It has to be remembered that all the male characters in the plays are not fops. A distinction has to be made between characters such as Mirabell and Valentine and the Tattles and Sir Fopling Flutters. The effeminate tones of the latter would be quite inappropriate for such virile characters as Mirabell, Valentine and Mr. Horner.

Perhaps the most difficult task for an actor playing one of these parts is to sustain his zest and comedy attack throughout the play and, at the same time, to keep on top of the exacting vocal technique. Let us look at part of a speech by Mrs. Sullen in Act Two of Farquhar's *The Beaux Stratagem*:

"Country pleasures! Racks and torments! Dost think, child, that my limbs were made for leaping of ditches and clambering over stiles? Or that my parents, wisely foreseeing my future happiness in country pleasures, had early instructed me in rural accomplishments of drinking fat ale, playing at whisk, and smoking tobacco with my husband? Or of spreading of plasters, brewing of diet-drinks, and stilling rosemary-water, with the good old gentlewoman my mother-in-law?

Not that I disapprove of rural pleasures, as the poets have painted them: in their landscape, every Phyllis has her Corydon; every murmuring stream and every flowery mead gives fresh alarms to love. Besides, you'll find, that their couples were never married. But yonder I see my Corydon, and a sweet swain it is, Heaven knows!"

The chief danger here is for the player to make Mrs. Sullen sound sarcastic or bad-tempered. This would destroy the comedy as she would lose the sympathy of the audience. She is enjoying her description of rural pursuits. The tone is set by her first words "Country pleasures! Racks and torments!" The contrast between "pleasures" and "torments" has to be brought out by contrasted inflections. And then the words "leaping" and "clambering" are there to be used colourfully. If Mrs. Sullen imagines herself jumping over a rustic, ill-made stile in her long skirts, as she says the words, it will help her to get the right tone-colour. She now elaborates her ideas and the next section, from "Oh that my parents" down to "mother-in-law", can be taken fast and lightly.

But her scorn of all things rural needs to come out on the words "fat ale" and "whisk" (a card game). It was fashionable to be bored by one's husband in Restoration times and so "smoking tobacco with my husband" calls for "a dying fall" and a suggestion of the tediousness of this occupation. She is obviously not enamoured of the good works she has to undertake - "spreading of plasters, brewing of diet-drinks, stilling rosemary-water" - and this distaste has to be expressed, but she should not sound contemptuous of "the good old gentlewoman" her mother-in-law. A Les Dawson crack at the expense of the music-hall figure of the mother-in-law should be avoided.

Now comes a complete change of subject which calls for a lift of the voice, "Not that I disapprove of country pleasures as the poets have painted them." "Poets" is the key word here - best emphasised by a compound inflection. Now she is really enjoying herself,

"In their landscape, every Phyllis has her Corydon, every murmuring stream and every flowery mead, gives fresh alarms to love".

A mock romantic style would be appropriate as she makes fun of the pastoral convention with its shepherds and shepherdesses. The sudden drop to reality on "Besides, you'll find that their couples were never married" should get a laugh. "Their" and "married" being the key words. The last phrases need careful handling with the word "my" being pointed, "But yonder I see my Corydon, and a sweet swain it is, Heaven knows." How Mrs. Sullen speaks the last words depends on her interpretation of the part and on her attitude to her husband.

*Accessories*

Mrs. Sullen might well use a fan. Accessories were toys to high society: the fans, handkerchiefs, canes, muffs, snuff-boxes. There were seventeen different movements which were used when taking snuff and many different moods could be expressed by the sniff: such as military, contemptuous or polite.

The fan had a language of its own. The charming essay by Joseph Addison entitled *The Fan Exercise* which is supposedly a letter written to *The Spectator* by the Principal of an Academy "for the training up of young women in the exercise of the Fan according to the most fashionable airs and motions that are now practised at court", has already been mentioned. He gives a detailed description of the various exercises in the use of a fan: *Handling the Fan, Grounding the Fan* and *Fluttering the Fan*.

The account of *Fluttering the Fan* would form the basis of a useful exercise for anyone playing in Restoration Comedy:

" . . . There is the angry flutter, the confused flutter, and the amorous flutter . . . there is scarce any emotion in the mind which does not produce a suitable agitation in the fan; in so much that if I only see the fan of a disciplined lady, I know very well whether she laughs, frowns, or blushes. I have seen a fan so very angry, that it would have been dangerous if the absent lover who provoked it were to have come within the wind of it; and at other times, so very languishing, that I have been glad for the lady's sake the lover was at a sufficient distance from it . . . a fan is either a prude or coquette according to the nature of the person who bears it."

The movement of the fan has to be motivated, as indeed, all movement and gesture has to be in Restoration Comedy.

So often one sees actors in these plays waving their arms about pointlessly, having no regard to what they are saying at the time. However, the fops, who were laughed at because they aped the manners of the 'heroes' and overdid it, can make more exaggerated gestures than the other characters.

### Costume and its Effect On Movement

The costume and accessories, of course, affect the movement. Wearing a periwig, handling a sword, a cane, a lace handkerchief or a fan all present problems and have to be carefully rehearsed.

A common mistake is to keep the elbows in too close to the sides when making a gesture. The sleeves, it is true, were tight-fitting to the elbow but much was made of the movement of the forearms and the wrists. Indeed, a lady's forearm was considered to be one of her most attractive features. When the lace at the elbow fell back, it framed the lower part of the arm and revealed its charms. The man's calf was considered to be a particularly pleasing feature and so a turned out position of the feet was adopted whether the man was standing or sitting. The wig can cause problems when the character turns his head. An actor's face has been known to disappear entirely into the side of his wig because he turned his head too sharply. He should not stand too much in profile to the audience during the performance of a Restoration play, lest his wig obscures his features.

*The Attitude to the Plays*

Perhaps the worst pitfall of all for the actor in Restoration Comedy is to superimpose on it the attitudes and social customs of the twentieth century: to stand apart from the plays as if to say aren't these people quaint? or aren't they outrageous? The player has to bring to the great plays of the Restoration Period a vitality, an elegance and ease which matches the wit and grace of the dialogue.

## Late Eighteenth Century Comedy

The four most frequently revived plays of the late eighteenth century are *The Critic*, *The Rivals*, *The School for Scandal*, and *She Stoops to Conquer*. They all make strenuous demands on the director and cast. The most complete fulfilment of these demands that I have ever witnessed was in the quarrel scene in *The School for Scandal* between Sir Peter and Lady Teazle, as played by Laurence Olivier and Vivien Leigh.

She looked exquisite, a porcelain figure, delicate, graceful, alternating a bubbling sense of fun with a teasing mischievousness. There was affection for her husband behind even her most provoking remarks,

"If you wanted authority over me, you should have adopted me, and not married me: I am sure you were old enough."

and,

**Lady Teazle:**

Well, then, there is but one thing more you can make me to add to the obligation, and that is -

**Sir Peter:**

My widow, I suppose.

**Lady Teazle:**

Hem! Hem!

The actress playing Lady Teazle has to remember that Sir Peter is in a vulnerable position: he is much older than his wife. She has the capacity to wound him if she plays the scene without affection. This will alienate the audience. On more than one occasion, I have seen a Lady Teazle who was played more like Katherina in *The Taming of the Shrew* than Sheridan's delightful creation. An unkind, malicious Lady Teazle kills the good-natured comedy of the scene. One has to remember that she is unlike the rest of the scandal-mongering circle, because she is essentially good-hearted.

Olivier played Sir Peter with a gentle sense of comedy and with a charm equal to that of his spouse. He was a perfect foil to her quicksilver vitality. The scene was a delight to the eye as well as to the ear. As Vivien Leigh moved across the stage swiftly and impulsively, all fluttering silks and ribbons, I thought of Hugh Thompson's exquisite, colour-plates illustrating the play. Sir Peter's supposed age was suggested by Olivier without any clichéd shakes or tottering steps.

I was reminded of Olivier's performance by Michael Bryant, playing a different part in a different play. His Mr. Hardcastle in *She Stoops to Conquer* had the same genial charm and ease. When he said,

"I love everything that's old: old books, old wives"

he created the whole character of Hardcastle in a mellow mood. One was aware that here was an actor completely on top of the technique needed for the part. One was conscious too of hidden reserves of strength in his characterisation. And when he had to show anger and indignation later on in the play, he was equally convincing.

Dora Bryan appeared as Mrs. Hardcastle in the same National Theatre production. Although I must admit that some of this performance went beyond the bounds of credibility, she looked magnificent and wore the period costume with a great sense of style. Her hands were used eloquently. She created an irresistibly comic moment and raised the biggest laugh of the evening when, in response to her husband's line,

"So now to supper, tomorrow we shall gather all the poor of the parish about us"

she said, "Oh" in a tone of great repugnance, accompanied by an expression of extreme distaste. Voice, facial expression and timing all came together and this shock of the unexpected produced the audience's delighted reaction.

Andrew C. Wadsworth, who played Tony Lumpkin, gave a performance distinguished by a remarkable sense of spontaneity. He seemed to be genuinely enjoying the situation at the start of the play when he sent Marlow and Hastings to the supposed inn - the Hardcastle house. His lines appeared to be freshly thought.

I always have sympathy for anyone cast in the thankless part of Constance. I had to play this 'stick' of a girl at RADA and found it difficult to bring her to life. But so long as the actress playing her provides a contrast to the more lively character of Kate and remains in period, resisting the temptation to try to do too much with the part, she should serve the production well.

The part of Lydia Languish in Sheridan's *The Rivals* affords great opportunities to the actress. The name gives the clue to the characterisation. Sheridan is making fun of the romantic young lady of the period, who spends her leisure time reading the romances from the circulating library. This is a character part too often played straight. Lydia's movement should suggest a languid personality, revealed in her way of handling a shawl, of holding a book. A slight drawl would be appropriate, provided that it did not slow her down too much.

She is a delicious little goose. Her comic distress when she realises that she is not to elope with Beverley but to have,

"a regular humdrum wedding"

needs to be conveyed with a light but firm touch, and perhaps a little self-mockery,

"Oh, that I should live to hear myself called Spinster!"

# The Comedy of Oscar Wilde

Over a hundred years separates the plays of Oscar Wilde from those of Sheridan and Goldsmith. We find the same Irish wit in Wilde but, especially in *The Importance of Being Earnest*, more surface glitter.

The dialogue is diamond sharp: epigrams and paradoxes abound. The style resembles that of the earlier Congreve. However, we are now in a completely different age, the last years of Queen Victoria's reign, the *fin de siècle*. Instead of the open licentiousness of Restoration society we find upper class hypocrisy. This hypocrisy is amusingly handled in Wilde's masterpiece, *The Importance of Being Earnest*, but he has a heavier touch in *Lady Windermere's Fan* and *An Ideal Husband*.

His 'good' women are difficult to play convincingly. The actress has to steer a tricky course between sounding like a cold prig on the one hand and like a heroine in melodrama on the other. Take Lady Windermere's speech at the beginning of Act Three when she is waiting for Lord Darlington in his rooms, as an example. This begins,

"Why doesn't he come? This waiting is horrible"

and ends,

"I have heard that men are brutal, horrible . . ."

Today's actresses find it difficult to imagine Lady Windermere's agony of mind. The heightened language is an embarrassment. The safest way to play the speech is with real emotion, but to play it down a little. If there is a hint of melodrama in the delivery, the lines will get a laugh.

The 'bad' character in the play, Mrs. Erlynne has a difficult scene to play with her daughter, in which she begs her to go back to Lord Windermere. She has a long speech, written in a florid, rhetorical style, which calls for tact and control. If it is built up very gradually to the climax at the end, and if a quiet intensity is used for the earlier part, much of the danger inherent in the style will be avoided. Above all, the actress must appear to believe in every word that she is saying.

When playing in Wildean comedy, and particularly in *The Importance of Being Earnest,* it is vital to speak the text with complete accuracy. Even a syllable out of place will destroy the balance and rhythm of the carefully constructed dialogue. Charm is not valued very much today as part of an actor's armoury. However, the parts of Algernon and Jack both demand this attribute, although their characters are not otherwise alike.

Edith Evans' portrayal of Lady Bracknell has long been regarded as definitive, but there are signs of a new approach to the part. Younger actresses are being cast in the rôle and finding different interpretations, even of the famous handbag line and Judi Dench brought a fresh approach to the part with notable success. More recently, Maggie Smith's performance has delighted both critics and audiences.

## The Comedy of Nöel Coward

Just as Edith Evans stamped the part of Lady Bracknell with her own inimitable style, so has Nöel Coward stamped the parts that he wrote for himself with his personality. His clipped, staccato speech perfectly matched his epigrammatical dialogue. While his performances remain in the memory of playgoers, anyone taking on Coward parts in revivals has a formidable task.

An imitation of 'The Master's' vocal technique is unwise, but a great deal can be learned from his timing and changes of tempi in his famous recording of the balcony love-scene with Gertrude Lawrence in *Private Lives.* This only took an hour to record, but is an object lesson in the exact use of pause and inflection:

| | |
|---|---|
| **Elyot:** | I went round the world you know after - |
| **Amanda:** | Yes, yes, I know. How was it? |
| **Elyot:** | The world? |
| **Amanda:** | Yes. |
| **Elyot:** | Oh, highly enjoyable |

| Amanda: | China must be very interesting. |
|---|---|
| Elyot: | Very big, China. |
| Amanda: | And Japan - |
| Elyot: | Very small." |

Nöel Coward has described *Private Lives* as "the lightest of comedies, based on a serious situation, which is two people who love each other too much . . . there's sadness below it." This is frequently true of the best kind of comedy. It is present in Charlie Chaplin's films and in the plays of Alan Ayckbourn. An actor who plays *Private Lives* on a purely superficial level misunderstands the playwright's intention.

As one would expect from a working actor who had been in the theatre since childhood, learning the business even in those early days with a down-to-earth professionalism, Nöel Coward had some wise things to say about the technique of playing comedy. He advised actors to learn how to control an audience, to kill small laughs in order to get a much bigger laugh later on. "Don't let the audience rule you" he said, "rule them."

He was a past-master of the throw-away line. When he played Henry Gow in *Fumed Oak* he got enormous laughs on these lines, which he never 'plugged':

"I should also like to take this opportunity of saying that I hate that bloody awful slave bangle and I always have."

"Here, see this ham? That's what I think of the ham. *(He throws it at her feet.)* And the tomatoes and the A1 bloody sauce!" *(He throws them too.)*

Playing in Coward is a demanding discipline for actors.

## Playing in Farce

*"Farce is tragedy without the dignity."*
Ben Travers

Farce is generally recognized as being the most difficult style of acting to bring off successfully. There are one or two brilliant farceurs today, but only one or two. And, indeed, historically, the great farce actors have been few and far be-

116

tween. One of these was Ralph Lynn, described by Ben Travers as the most accomplished timer he had ever known. I count myself fortunate enough to have worked with both Ben Travers and Ralph Lynn in the revivals of some of their Aldwych successes. Ralph Lynn directed most of these revivals himself. He was a meticulous and exacting director. A brilliant timer himself, he tried to inculcate this sense of timing in his cast. He would say that,

"A performance has a rhythm from the opening lines to the final ones and you must never miss a beat. This rhythm goes through everything - the actual lines you speak, the pauses, the moves, the turn of the head, the stage-business."

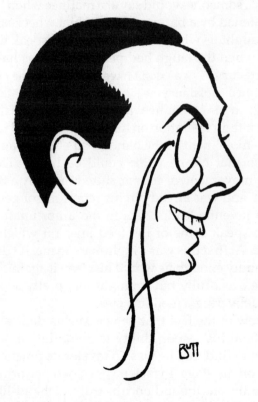

Figure 3: A Caricature of Ralph Lynn

Peter O'Toole used to come to the matinées when Lynn was playing at the Duke of York's Theatre, to watch his timing. I believe that it was generally an instinctive thing with him, but he also worked very hard to perfect stage-business such as the drop of his monocle to point a line. He demanded split second timing of exits and entrances and woe-betide you if you mistimed one.

He was adept at timing laughs. Members of the company would stand in the wings listening to him controlling an audience's reactions. When we were playing to a house afflicted by coughs and sneezes he seemed able to anticipate when these were going to come on the key word. "Listen to Ralph tripping the coughs", someone would say at a matinée when the dialogue was threatened by a barrage of bronchial wheezes.

He taught us when to cut a laugh and speak the next line. This was when the laugh had peaked and was halfway on its downward curve - "You don't have to wait until the man in the circle has finished explaining the joke to his dear Aunt Mabel." At this latter stage in his career he was troubled with huskiness in his voice, despite an operation on his vocal cords, and used to make a nervous movement of the hand to quieten the audience after a laugh so that his next line could be heard. This nervous, fluttering movement, of course, suited the 'silly ass' characters he played, and was already in his repertoire of gestures.

As a juvenile lead, I was in the unfortunate position of having to speak some of the feed lines on which his laughs depended. At first this was a nightmare to me. If I did not speak the line loudly enough he would hiss 'say it again'. This embarrassed me dreadfully but it taught me, pretty soon, the technique of delivering a feed line clearly.

In view of the fact that he was such a dedicated actor, so serious about his responsibility to an audience, it was rather surprising to find that he was an inveterate practical joker and ad-libber on the stage. In fact, he gave two performances at the same time: the one the audience heard; and the ad-libbed one for the benefit of the cast, delivered with fiendish ingenuity under cover of the laughs. But he read the riot act to anyone who

118

'corpsed' - came out of character - and laughed during a performance. When *Outrageous Fortune*, the last play Ben Travers wrote for Ralph Lynn and Robertson Hare, came to the Winter Garden Theatre, Robertson Hare, who cracked easily, begged Ralph not to make him laugh, particularly when we knew that other actors were in the audience. This, of course, was fatal and merely had the effect of egging him on.

I think Ralph used these ad-libs to get the adrenalin flowing and to keep his performance fresh over a long run. This side of him was particularly unexpected as he always stressed the importance in farce acting of apparently taking everything seriously. Both Lynn and Travers were scornful of actors who indulged in nods and winks at the audience as if to say - look at me, I'm being funny.

Farce has been described as "real people in unreal situations." This is a helpful definition as it underlines the need for the characters to be believable, so that the audience can identify with them. Human nature being what it is, it is pleasurable to laugh at other people's misfortunes, to watch them suffer, particularly if the character is likeable. Personal charm is a great asset to the farceur - it enables him to get away with behaviour which, if looked at coldly, could be considered boorish, stupid and even offensive.

The plot of many farces revolves around the confrontation of the chief character with a female dragon. This is usually his wife, but sometimes a local dignitary or the daily woman. Even the dragons in farce should not be played viciously or over played so that they become unbelievable as characters.

Ralph used to tell us, at rehearsals, about Mary Brough, one of the Aldwych team, who made a great success as the daily woman in *Rookery Nook*. He said that she broke all the rules of technique, muddled up her lines, mistimed her exit, but invariably went off to the accompaniment of the biggest round of applause in the play. Audiences loved her, her empurpled, angry, turkey-cock face and her incoherent, outraged dignity. Ben Travers wrote her character's dialogue with her personality in mind. Some of her lines became catchphrases. Robertson

Figure 4: Ralph Lynn and Robertson Hare in *Outrageous Fortune* by Ben Hare. Photograph by Denis de Marney

Hare, in his book *Yours Indubitably*, tells of a conversation he had with George VI,

> "'How long have you been in your profession, Mr. Hare?' he asked. I replied that I had started in 1912. 'Earlier than that I cannot be, as Mary Brough would have said', the King remarked."

*What are the basic rules of farce acting?*

1) The actor must appear to believe in the situation and to take it seriously. Confiding in the audience, as if to say 'You and I know that this play is ridiculous, but let's have a good laugh', is fatal. Shakespeare, in Hamlet's advice to the Players, shows that he knows all about actors who do this,

> " ... there be of them that will themselves laugh, to set on some quantity of barren spectators to laugh too, though in the meantime some necessary question of the play be then to be considered."

2) The actor must keep the rhythm of the play flowing.

3) The actor must be able to time his laughs.

4) The actor must be able to communicate everything clearly to the audience and especially feed lines upon which the next section of dialogue depends.

5) The actor must make it all look easy and natural. A common fault in farce acting is forcing. The actor works too hard, using an overloud voice, over-emphatic delivery of lines and exaggerated facial expression. Frequently, the characterisation is allowed to go over the top. Funny walks and funny accents should be eschewed.

6) The actor has to sustain vitality and pace. He has to keep a 'bubble of fun' inside him. C. E. Montague, the great drama critic, said of one of the greatest farce actors, Coquelin,

> "His power was simply the sum of the true strict elements of great acting - a plastic physical medium, a finished technical cunning and *a passion of joy in the thought of the character acted*." (Author's italics)

Who are the good farce actors today? Among them, Richard Briers comes immediately to mind. He has the charm and necessary technique, he suffers convincingly. Alec Guinness gave a remarkable performance in Feydeau's *Hôtel Paradiso*. Griff Rhys Jones' performance in *Charley's Aunt* (appropriately at the Aldwych Theatre) was true to the best traditions of farce. As well as preserving the traditional comedy business, he brought comic inventiveness to the part when, for example, he drank a glassful of plonk.

Bernard Cribbins gave a resourceful performance as the foil to Richard Briers in Ray Cooney's farce, *Run For Your Wife*. Ray Cooney himself, in *It Runs in the Family*, demonstrated his understanding of the essential elements required for successfully acting in this genre.

Who are the bad actors in farce? Their name is legion and shall be anonymous.

# Chapter Eight

# Pinter and After

" . . . to hold, as 'twere, the mirror up to nature; to show virtue
her own feature, scorn her own image, and the very age
and body of the time his form and pressure."
*Hamlet*

The old, stereotypical stage-world of elegant drawing-
rooms, gracious, flower-arranging hostesses and tennis-play-
ing youth was swept away in the mid nineteen-fifties by John
Osborne's *Look Back In Anger*. Kenneth Tynan described this
ground-breaking play as "the best young play of its decade." John
Osborne was a revolutionary in that he gave post-war youth a
voice; he spoke for a generation of state-aided University students. *Look Back In Anger* is regarded as a landmark, a water-
shed in theatrical history.

## Harold Pinter

The fact that Harold Pinter was also revolutionary is often overlooked. He, too, broke new ground. He had the courage to place the inarticulate at the centre of his plays and he brought a poet's ear to the creation of apparently naturalistic dialogue.

Before Pinter arrived on the scene, the main characters in plays were usually educated and eloquent. Jimmy Porter's flow of words is a typical example. Pinter's characters speak quite differently - in short, broken sentences, full of hesitations and repetitions. He has had a tremendous influence on the way that actors think, move and speak; and on playwrights too. There has been a good deal of sub-Pinteresque playwriting since the sixties. The influence persists. But the acting style demanded by Pinter is not easy to achieve nor is his skill in writing dialogue.

## Pinter's Dialogue

Pinter is a poet, an actor and a writer. Because of these three talents he has developed an unique style. He has a selective ear for colloquial speech and speech rhythms. His words come easily off the page - in other words, the lines are speakable. However, he is not an actor-proof playwright. Unless the director and actor understand the subtext of underlying feeling, the dramatic impact of the words will be lost.

At one time, Pinter's one-act plays were very popular with amateur dramatic societies, but seldom with their audiences. This was due to a variety of reasons. The principal one was that in their endeavour to act in a 'natural' way, the actors were not projecting their voices and the audience could not hear what they were saying. Secondly, the directors were not always clear in their minds as to what underlay the dialogue, so that the necessary charge of strong emotion was lacking.

Thirdly, Pinter's essential pauses were neglected and pauses were made where he did not intend them. This was fatal to the rhythm of the dialogue and to the dramatic momentum of the play. I have, however, seen one or two very good productions of Pinter's one-acters by amateurs who have had a perceptive director, one who had thought seriously about the characters' motives and inner conflicts.

## Pauses in Pinter's Dialogue

Observing the famous 'Pinter Pause' is vital. Peter Hall, a fine director of his plays, has worked closely with the playwright and has said that if you neglect a comma in the script, you do so at your peril. Indeed he has held 'pause rehearsals' in which the actors have studied the indications in the text as to length of pause. These vary from "..." (a short pause), to "*Pause*" (a longer one) and "*Silence*" (a very long one).

It may be apocryphal, but Pinter is alleged to have shouted at the actors in a rehearsal, "You're playing two dots at the moment, and I think, if you'll check in the script, you'll find it's three." These pauses should never be dead. Enough energy has to be generated in the preceding words to carry the actors through the time until the next line is spoken.

To use an analogy - in the days before thermostatically controlled irons were in use, the current had to be switched off from time to time in order that the iron should not become overheated and scorch the material. But there had to be enough heat left in it to last until the next stage of the ironing had been completed. And enough charge of emotional pressure has to be built up before the pause, in order to sustain the dramatic tension before the next line is spoken.

Pinter's short sketch, *The Black and the White*, provides a striking example of this:

| | |
|---|---|
| **1st Old Woman:** | You can see what goes on from this top table. (*Pause*) It's better than going down to that place on the embankment, anyway. |
| **2nd Old Woman:** | Yes, there's not too much noise. |
| **1st Old Woman:** | There's always a bit of noise. |
| **2nd Old Woman:** | Yes, there's always a bit of life. |
| | (*Pause*) |

| | |
|---|---|
| **1st Old Woman:** | They'll be closing down soon to give it a scrub round. |
| **2nd Old Woman:** | There's a wind out. |
| | *(Pause)* |
| **1st Old Woman:** | I wouldn't mind staying. |

Unless they both visualise what it is going to feel like to be turned out into the cold, windy streets after the milk bar closes, the impact of "There's a wind out" and "I wouldn't mind staying" will be lost.

The apparently realistic language is carefully crafted, particularly in its use of rhythm and repetition. It is not for nothing that his style has been called rhapsodic and emotional. There's "magic in the web of it."

## Repetition

Pinter sometimes uses repetition to show the inability of a character to express himself in precise terms, as is shown here in *The Dumb Waiter*,

"I was thinking about that girl, that's all. She wasn't much to look at, I know, but still. It was a mess though, wasn't it? What a mess. Honest, I can't remember a mess like that one. They don't seem to hold together like men. A looser texture like. Didn't she spread, eh? She didn't half spread."

## Technical Devices

The actor who plays in Pinter needs to know and understand the technical devices he repeatedly uses. He often puts two characters in opposition, one quicker in the uptake and more forceful than the other. Gus and Ben in *The Dumb Waiter* are typical examples. If the two actors use contrasted pace and pitch, the conflict will be brought out. But if they sound alike, the dialogue, obviously, will be flattened.

Another device Pinter often employs is to introduce a sudden note of menace into an ordinary domestic situation. In *The Birthday Party* a game of Blind Man's Bluff is in progress.

126

Then there is a sudden blackout, during which we hear a child's drum being kicked around the room. The atmosphere becomes threatening, violence erupts.

The actor has to be ready for these dislocating changes of mood. They may be shown in words or in physical violence. In either case they have to be strongly projected. When the envelope is pushed under the door in *The Dumb Waiter* the two actors need to react strongly to this invasion of their closed world: their security is threatened.

## Communication

Communication with the audience is especially important when playing in Pinter, because the text itself is sometimes obscure. One of Pinter's themes is the failure of people to communicate with each other. But that does not exonerate the actor from communicating with the audience.

## Alan Bennett

Alan Bennett's satirical gift was displayed early on when that remarkable revue *Beyond the Fringe* came to London in 1960 and launched the careers of the four young men who made up the company - Alan Bennett, Jonathan Miller, Dudley Moore and Peter Cook. Harold Hobson described Bennett as apparently the mildest, but in reality the most lethal of the four. He has a wickedly accurate ear for the tones of voice of clergymen, "now Esau was an hairy man", and schoolmasters.

The scene in *Forty Years On* in which he played a young master explaining the facts of life to a boy, was keenly observed, controlled and intensely funny:

"Well, Foster, what I want you to tackle now is this problem of your body."

He did not allow the satire to become caricature. His talent has continued to develop both in his work for the stage and for television. His monologues, *Talking Heads*, are masterpieces of their kind and his two stage plays, *Single Spies*, were successfully adapted for television.

He is a caring playwright, deeply concerned with the still, sad music of humanity and with realism. The actor in a play by Bennett must avoid self-pity. There is a North Country stoicism about many of Bennett's characters. Because he achieves some of his most powerful emotional effects by the use of implication, rather than by direct statement, the actor needs to explore the subtext without losing the naturalness of the apparently trivial words.

There is an example of Bennett's style in a television play he called *A Woman of no Importance*, borrowing the title from Wilde. Patricia Routledge gave a fine performance in it, which was at times harrowing to watch. She played a lonely woman who finds comfort in the trivia of office life and who is operated on for cancer and subsequently dies. The word cancer is never mentioned, but we pick up clues as the play proceeds:

"I bethought me of the bed-jacket Miss Brunskill had knitted me. I had put it away in my locker because she'd made it too tight round the sleeves, but I tried it on again and it was just right."

"I've started coming and looking out of this window, I just find it far enough"

and

"I keep wondering about my Dad."

Bennett constantly moves from tragedy to comedy. It is essential that the actor displays as much tact in performing the scripts as Bennett does in the writing of them and is equally sensitive to nuances of feeling. Alan Bennett has a nostalgia for the past and a love of England. He demonstrated this vividly in *Forty Years On*, although the manner of expression appeared flippant and satirical. The actor has to be ready for what lies under the apparently cool and laid-back comic satire and for the complex shifts of mood.

But the dialogue is rewarding to speak. Like Pinter, Bennett has an ear for the give and take of ordinary conversation. And so he does much of the work for the actor, if the actor trusts him. One sometimes hears the dialogue submerged by an over-emphatic delivery or by an obtrusive use of an accent.

Alan Bates and Coral Browne, in Alan Bennett's television drama *An Englishman Abroad,* gave an object lesson in how to speak Bennett's dialogue:

| | |
|---|---|
| **Burgess:** | How do you like Moscow? |
| **Coral:** | Loathe it. I cannot understand what those three sisters were on about. It gives the play a very sinister start. |
| **Burgess:** | A Scotch would help. |
| **Coral:** | Haven't you had enough? If you're not at the Embassy what do you do? |
| **Burgess:** | Liaise. |
| **Coral:** | Press? |
| **Burgess:** | Sort of. |
| **Coral:** | You're not feeling sick again? |
| **Burgess:** | I think I am rather. |
| **Coral:** | Oh God. |
| **Burgess:** | One of the few lessons I have learned in life is that when one is sick it is always in threes. |

When Coral Browne is asked to order a suit for Burgess from his former tailors in the West End, the dialogue runs as follows:

| | |
|---|---|
| **Coral:** | I'd like to order some suits. |
| **Tailor:** | Certainly, Madam. |
| **Coral:** | You've made suits for the gentleman before, but he now lives abroad. |
| **Tailor:** | I see. |
| **Coral:** | I took his measurements. I'm not sure they're . . . |
| **Tailor:** | Could one know the gentleman's name? |
| **Coral:** | Yes. Mr. Burgess. |
| **Tailor:** | We have two Mr. Burgess's. I take it that this is Mr. Burgess G? How is Mr. Burgess? Fatter, I see. One of our more colourful customers. Too little colour in our drab lives these days. |

Nigel Hawthorne was impeccable as the tailor. He allowed the dialogue and situation to carry the comedy, but put a depth of understanding underneath his delivery of the apparently conventional words.

What kind of qualities then does the actor in a play by Alan Bennett need? Certainly the North Country characteristics of honesty, directness and, sometimes, bluntness. The essential truthfulness in Bennett's approach has to be reflected in the acting. As he says himself, "Acting is a painful business and it's to do with exposure not concealment." He was aware that when Kenneth More played the main character in *Getting On*, his desire to be liked by the audience meant that the character was not truly developed. And one of the reasons for the playwright's obvious regard for the work of Coral Browne was surely that he recognised the directness and integrity which characterised her approach to a role.

In addition to a down-to-earth honesty, the actor has to be able to convey subtle shades of feeling through casual seeming, colloquial dialogue: whether it be the love for a vanished England in *Forty Years On*; or the heartbreak behind the gallant cheerfulness of the dying woman in *A Woman of No Importance*.

## Peter Shaffer

Peter Shaffer has an astonishing track record and continues to add to it. His plays have appeared at regular intervals and the list is impressive: *Amadeus*; *The Battle of the Shrivings*; *Black Comedy*; *Equus*; *Five Finger Exercise*; *The Gift of the Gorgon*; *Lettice and Lovage*; *The Private Ear*; *The Public Eye*; *The Royal Hunt of the Sun*; *The White Liars*; and *Yonadab*.

Actors and directors have always wanted to work with him because he provides meaty parts and stimulating challenges for them. In recent years, he has asked for more and more from his designers as he has moved from the comparatively simple domestic setting for *Five Finger Exercise* to the much more complicated *mise en scènes* of *Amadeus* and *Yonadab*.

Shaffer has received praise from the critics and also accusations that his work is superficial and depends too much on staging and stage effects. Few of them, however, have denied that among the reasons for his success are the dramatic impact of his work and its accessibility to the public. My chief concern here is with the actor's approach to the plays.

## Shaffer's Dialogue

Shaffer gives his characters long speeches, full of imagery and colour. They demand large-scale acting. The actor needs a flexible voice with a wide range of pitch. He has to be able to 'see' the imagery and to convey this vision by the tone-colour in his voice. He has to be able to shape the speeches to their major and minor climaxes and to sustain his mental and vocal vitality throughout.

Here are some examples of the demands Peter Shaffer makes on his actors. The image may be an extended one or the mere flash of an idea, such as when Clive, the son of the household, in *Five Finger Exercise*, is describing his family, in particular his pretentious mother, to Walter, the German tutor:

"Let us, therefore, not gasp too excitedly at the loftiness of mother's family tree. Unbeknownst to Father it has, as you see, roots of clay. Still they are French roots."

Two of the most effective uses of imagery occur at the end of Dysart's final speech in *Equus*, in which the psychiatrist examines and questions the nature of his work:

"And I? I stand in the dark, with a pick in my hand, striking at heads!" and,

"There is now in my mouth, this sharp chain. And it never comes out."

In the long speeches the actor is helped by the rhythmical way in which Shaffer writes. There is, also, a rhetorical use of repetition and antithesis. Bob, in *The Private Ear*, is entertaining a girl in his flat for the first time. He is intensely shy to begin with but, as the play develops, he becomes more eloquent:

"Do you know how many thousands of years it took to make anything so beautiful, so feeling, as your hand? People say I know something like the back of my hand, but they don't know their hands. They wouldn't recognise a photograph of them. Why? Because their hands are anonymous. They're just tools for filing invoices, turning lathes round. They cramp up from picking slag out of moving belts of coal."

Incidentally, in two of these examples there is a reference to coal mining. Shaffer was conscripted and worked as a coal miner from 1944 to 1947.

Sometimes there is, I think, some justification for the charge laid at Shaffer's door that the presentation is more interesting than the content of his plays. Looking back on the production I saw of *Equus*, my most vivid memory is of the horses, played by actors each wearing the metal outline of a horse's head. The quintessence of a horse was suggested by the carriage of their heads and necks and by the poise and controlled movements of their bodies. The effect of their metal hooves striking the stage was dramatic. I can see now the dignity and grace of those movements.

On the other hand, although *Amadeus* was presented with a stunning stage setting, portraying the court of Vienna in Mozart's day, it did not detract from the central situation - the tragedy of Salieri and his venomous hostility to Mozart. Here we saw the contrast between the two. Salieri, the chaste-living man, whom God had endowed with the ability to recognise genius but with only a second-rate talent, was juxtaposed to a giggling, scatological youth, endowed with God-given genius.

The strength of this central idea gives the actor playing Salieri a wonderful opportunity (which Paul Scofield grasped with both hands) to express a corroding, jealous bitterness. And Shaffer has given him the words to work with,

"Tonight, at an inn somewhere in this city, stands a giggling child who can put on paper, without actually setting down his billiard cue, casual notes which turn my most considered ones into lifeless scratches. Grazie Signore! . . . You put into me perception of the Incomparable - which most men never know - then ensured that I would know myself for ever mediocre."

It requires considerable vocal technique to do justice to Shaffer's language. Many of the speeches are passionate, and profound feeling has to be expressed without the use of over-loud volume or prolonged periods of shouting. Intensity is a useful way of expressing the bitterness of Salieri.

Shaffer is not always wearing his high boots. In the part of Yonadab, he gave Alan Bates the opportunity to put over dry comedy in brief, cynical asides and, in *Lettice and Lovage*, he created a light comedy part in which Maggie Smith had great success both in London and New York.

## Tom Stoppard

Stoppard's style is in complete contrast to Shaffer's and demands very different acting skills. Young actors seem to find his dialogue easier to handle than either Bennett's or Shaffer's. His wit strikes sparks off them. For instance, I am always surprised to find how quickly students are able to identify with *Rosencrantz and Guildenstern*. The quick repartee and laid-back attitude of the pair strike an immediate chord.

Stoppard is often accused of being heartless, but this is to misjudge him. Even before he wrote *The Real Thing* he was concerned with human frailty and insecurity. In *Jumpers*, Dotty has strong emotional speeches about the disillusioning effect that the moon-landings have on her:

"Years and years ago, before a moon-landing seemed imminent at all, I thought, I felt that the destruction of moon mythology and moon association in poetry and romance, superstition and every-thing would be a sort of minute lobotomy, performed on the human race, like a tiny laser making dead some part of the psyche."

And,

"It'll be just you and me under that old-fashioned, silvery, har-vest moon, occasionally blue, jumped over by cows, and coupleted by Junes, invariably shining on the one I love; well-known in Carolina, much loved in Allegheny, familiar in Vermont; *(the screw turning in her) Keats'* bloody moon! for what has made the sage or poet write but the fair paradise of nature's light. And *Milton's* bloody moon! rising in clouded majesty, at length apparent queen, unveiled her peerless light and o'er the dark her silver mantle threw. And *Shelley's* sodding maiden, with white fire laden, whom mortals call the - *(weeping)*. Oh yes, things were in place then!"

The actress has to unleash great depths of feeling at the climactic end of this.

## Stoppard's Use of Language

Stoppard takes delight in language, in the use of puns, paradoxes and word-play. He is a meticulous craftsman of dialogue and plot. For example, the apparently illogical, sur-realist opening scene of *After Magritte* is fully explained at the end of the play.

This delight in words has to be shared by the actor. He has to be able to speak rapidly in order to catch the playwright's, and the character's, agility of mind. Firm articulation is needed to do justice to the sinewy, often alliterative language. Sustained nervous vitality is demanded too.

Ivanov in *Every Good Boy Deserves Favour* has a speech which calls for a virtuoso performance:

"I've got a blue-arsed bassoon, a blue-tongued contra-bassoon, an organ grinder's chimpani, and the bass drum is in need of a dermatologist."

It continues to explode in a series of verbal fireworks. A sus-tained mental and vocal attack is needed.

## Characterisation

It is difficult to keep up a consistent characterisation throughout all the pyrotechnics. Some of the brilliant set-pieces may tempt the actor into delivering them 'straight' and out of the context of the scene. One such set-piece is Henry's speech in *The Real Thing* in which he likens the writing of a play to the construction of a cricket-bat:

"This thing here, which looks like a wooden club, is actually several pieces of particular wood cunningly put together in a certain way so that the whole thing is sprung, like a dance floor. It's for hitting cricket balls with. If you get it right, the cricket ball will travel two hundred yards in four seconds . . . What we're trying to do is to write cricket bats . . ."

Much of Stoppard's dialogue has to be delivered with great speed and precision. Here is Cocklebury-Smythe in full flow in one of his speeches in *Dirty Linen* in which he is describing how the Prime Minister offered him a peerage,

"'Stop making such a fuss - do you want a life-peerage, or don't you?' 'No, I don't,' I said to him, 'What with only a couple of bachelor cousins in line ahead, one of whom is an amateur parachutist and the other a seamstress in the Merchant Navy, I prefer to hang on for a chance of the real thing.'"

It is of course essential that the character does not appear to be aware that he is saying anything out of the ordinary. In fact, apparent sincerity, and even earnestness at times, are a *sine qua non* when Stoppard's characters are delivering themselves of witticisms and playing verbal tricks,

"never took semaphore as a sophomore, more's the pity."

## Movement

Movement has to be considered very carefully. Because the audience has its work cut out to follow every twist and turn in the dialogue, one should not confuse the issue further by giving them too much to take in visually.

When Stoppard uses visual effects to create comedy, for example, the balancing of the overhead electric light with a form of counterweight in *After Magritte*, the audience has to be given time to absorb what is happening.

## Problems and Pitfalls

1) If the actor does not understand the logic in a speech he will not be able to make the thought processes of the character clear to the audience. Therefore, he must explore the tortuous development of ideas during rehearsals. In the more complicated

passages he may have to use pauses to enable the audience to catch up, and also to suggest that he is thinking the lines freshly.

2) A possible pitfall for the actor is to rely too much on the wit of the dialogue to do his work for him. The lines still have to be put over with careful pointing, timing and clarity.

3) Stoppard sometimes builds a speech to a climax in a very short time. This calls for considerable, controlled energy. A good example of this kind of challenge is part of Moon's speech from *The Real Inspector Hound*. He is giving a rallying-cry to "stand-ins of the world":

"It will follow me to my grave and become my epitaph. Here lies Moon, the second string; where's Higgs? Sometimes I dream of revolution, a bloody *coup d'État* by the second rank - troupes of actors slaughtered by their understudies, magicians sawn in half by indefatigably smiling glamour girls - cricket teams wiped out by marauding bands of twelfth men . . . stand-ins of the world stand up!"

The actor has to guard against allowing the wit of the dialogue here to swamp his characterisation.

Stoppard's plays are not easy to direct because split-second timing has to be achieved with the words and stage-business. They are not easy to act in because of the technical control of voice and movement which they demand from the cast. But they do provide a stimulating challenge to directors and actors. The experience of working on a play by Stoppard will never be dull.

## Alan Ayckbourn

Alan Ayckbourn's dialogue raises fewer problems than that of either Pinter or Bennett because it is more explicit. He does more of the work for the actor. He can reproduce the give and take of the ordinary conversation of his characters. His short lines crackle with comedy and his longer speeches are rhythmical.

Although the genre may appear to be light comedy or farce there is a subtext. Ayckbourn is aware of the bleakness and desolation in the lives of people striving to cope with the problems arising from today's shifting, materialistic society. One of his recurrent themes is the stresses which lie beneath marital relationships. Although there is some satire in his work there is also compassion and a sense of unease. He is troubled by the loneliness and insecurity of his characters. Because of his ability to reveal their psychological make-up, he has been compared to Chekov. There are some signs in his later plays that his view of life is becoming bleaker. In *Time of My Life*, an element of bitterness has emerged. How then, should an actor approach the creation of a part in an Ayckbourn play?

## The Approach to Characterisation

Observation of the real-life background of the character is a pre-requisite. This will include a study of speech, movement, dress, social manners and attitude of mind. Improvisation exercises are useful. By putting the actor into parallel situations to those in the play, his knowledge of the psychology of the character can be extended. Group improvisations can be used to explore the relationships between the various characters. Accurate reactions are important. They must be psychologically truthful. From a technical point of view they are necessary to feed the comedy lines. Ayckbourn places people precisely in their social milieu. If the actor does not study this in detail, and from real life, a stereotype will result or, worse, a caricature.

## Handling the Dialogue

The dialogue has to be given lightness and pace, but at the same time the lines have to be pointed. If they miss their mark, the result will be an unintelligible gabble. All forms of emphasis should be used to point the lines (these have already been enumerated in the chapter on *Modulation*). The success or failure of the comedy lines will depend on getting the emphatic values right, on knowing which are the key words and having the ability to give them significance in different ways. Also, it is useful to master the technique of the throw-away line.

## The Approach to Scenes

In *Gosforth's Fête*, one of the five playlets under the umbrella title of *Confusions* there are two parts which are sometimes given a superficial, clichéd characterisation. These are the scoutmaster and the clergyman. An indication of how the actor has approached the part, or how he has been directed, is the way he is dressed. The scout uniform should only be slightly ridiculous. If, for example, the length of the shorts is exaggerated, one fears the worst - and usually gets it. If the parsonical voice of the clergyman is overdone, the result will be a 'stage clergyman' and reality will be lost. The more believable these two are as people, the more amusing they will be.

Sometimes the actor has to probe for the emotion underneath the conversational style. The scene from *Absent Friends* in which Diana is talking to a girl who is having an affair with her husband is funny and touching at the same time. Ayckbourn's comedy is on several different levels here. He is making fun of current habits of speech, "basically", "I mean". The situation itself has comic elements and he has given Diana some comedy lines:

"And he's such a bad liar. If he takes the trouble to tell me that he is going to a football match, at least he should choose a day when they're playing at home."

This particular speech calls for a subtle approach. If Diana is made to sound aggressive the comedy does not emerge. Her facial expression has to be judged exactly and the stage business accurately timed.

In the opening scene of the original West End production of *Absurd Person Singular*, a seemingly less serious situation was explored. Richard Briers and Bridget Turner gave beautifully observed performances as a husband and wife involved in the frenzied last-minute preparations for a party that they are giving for people who might prove to be of use to them. The comedy situation develops logically and carries the audience along with it. Underneath it all, however, are the nervous anxieties of the over-house-proud wife, trying desperately not to let her husband down; and the jittery agitation of the husband, which he tries to cover up by a forced cheerfulness.

**Sidney:**     Hello, hello. What are we up to out here, eh?

**Jane** *(without pausing in her work)***:** Just giving it a wipe.

**Sidney:**     Dear oh dear. Good gracious me. Does it need it? Like a battleship - just like a battleship. They need you in the Royal Navy.

**Jane** *(giggling)***:**     Silly . . .

**Sidney:**     Still raining I see

**Jane:**     Shut the door, it's coming in.

**Sidney:**     Cats and dogs. Dogs and cats. *(Striding to the centre of the room and staring up at his digital clock, in the 'fourth wall')* Eighteen-twenty-three *(consulting his watch)* Eighteen-twenty-three. Getting on. Seven minutes - they'll be here.

**Jane:**     Oh.

**Sidney:**     I've got a few games lined up.

**Jane:**     Games?

**Sidney:**     Just in case.

**Jane:**     Oh good.

**Sidney:**     I've made a parcel for Pass the Parcel, sorted out a bit of music for musical bumps and thought out a few forfeits.

**Jane:**     Good.

**Sidney:**     I've thought up some real devils.

In the part of Norman in the trilogy *The Norman Conquests*, Ayckbourn has created a rewarding, richly comic but extremely demanding part. Pitfalls abound. As the man is really unlikeable, cruel, cold and egocentric, it is necessary to invest him with as much casual charm as possible. He has to convince us that he can attract women. He must not lose too much of the sympathy of the audience. He needs a light touch, coupled with enormous energy. One redeeming feature of the character is his infectious enjoyment of words:

"The trouble is, I was born in the wrong body. Look at me. A gigolo trapped in a haystack."

He relishes, rather engagingly, his own jokes and puns and he should make the audience share in his pleasure. Here he is at the breakfast table in *Table Manners*:

"Now then, what shall I have? Puffa Puffa rice. Ah-ha. No Sunday papers. Dear, dear. Ah well I shall have to read my morning cereal."

He is an irrepressible character.

## Style

Harold Pinter, Alan Bennett, Peter Shaffer, Tom Stoppard and Alan Ayckbourn each have an individual style. When John Gielgud was asked to define the word 'style' he said,

"It is knowing what kind of play you are in."

One could add, and it is knowing what kind of playwright has created your character and written your dialogue.

# Chapter Nine

# Some Masters

"The achieve of, the mastery of the thing"
*Gerard Manley Hopkins*

It has been said that actors are sculptors in snow, but because we can read contemporary records of past performances, and whilst great acting lives in the memory of those who have seen it, actors have a kind of immortality. It is true that, now, we also have records of their work on film and video, but I am concerned in this chapter with live actors performing in front of live audiences in the theatre and with that mysterious communion between them.

My list of masters of their art and craft is subjective. It is based on extensive playgoing over a long period of time, but inevitably some masterly actors will be left out.

Sir John Gielgud has mentioned the occasional reward an actor feels

"in a moment or two of thrilling contact with a particularly responsive audience."

I am sure that the excitement of those moments is shared by actor and audience alike. Some of these moments are stored in my memory, from the time I saw my first major production up to the most recent theatrical experience.

My generation is lucky in that it has seen the greatest actors of the twentieth century in their prime: John Gielgud, Laurence Olivier, Ralph Richardson, Edith Evans, Peggy Ashcroft. But,

" . . . other spirits there are standing apart
Upon the forehead of the age to come."

And in order that this chapter shall not be a rehearsal of past triumphs only, I am going to jump ahead and start with two performances by much younger actors of today which have given me the authentic thrill produced by the recognition of great talent.

The first of these was by Griff Rhys Jones as Lord Fancourt Babberley in *Charley's Aunt*. This revived the best traditions of classic farce acting. What made him so effective was that his aunt, unlike that of some of his predecessors in the role, was obviously masculine, hating his black bonnet and petticoats and all the time longing for a stiff drink and a cigar. The moment I treasure most from that performance is his panic and agonised expression when he realised that he was to be left alone with the ladies after dinner,

"What will they *talk* about?"

Great performances are not, of course, confined to the legitimate theatre and the next was in a musical.

From the moment that Robert Lindsay made his first entrance as Bill Snibson in *Me and My Girl*, what can only be described as a shock wave hit the audience. This was a performance in which the technical skills of characterisation, song and dance were combined with a complete belief in the imagined situation. Out of many satisfying moments, the one I remember most vividly is the one in which he told his girl very quietly that he loved her.

But now, back to the beginning. My first heart-stopping experience of seeing great acting was when I was taken to the Manchester Opera House to see *Romeo and Juliet*. Gielgud was playing Romeo and the moment I remember most vividly is when he was told of Juliet's supposed death. He stood very still and after a pause said, very quietly,

"Is it e'en so? Then I defy you stars."

The whole tragedy of the play was encapsulated in those words and by the drop in the voice on the last phrase. This was only the first of several such moments which Gielgud's acting has indelibly stamped on my mind.

Visual effects can sometimes have as great an impact as words. Even now, I can see the turn of Gielgud's wrist at the end of his speech about the death of kings in *Richard II*,

" . . . for within the hollow crown
That rounds the mortal temple of a king
Keeps Death his court . . .
. . . and with a little pin
Bores through his castle wall, and farewell king!"

He had been very still throughout the speech and that movement of the hand on "Bores through his castle wall" had the effect of a shout. The absorbed stillness in the audience was absolute.

Ralph Richardson as Sir John Falstaff took everyone by storm. I recall, when he made his first entrance, the moment of delighted recognition that this was Shakespeare's Falstaff brought to exuberant life. And when, years later, I saw him in *The Double Dealer* at the National Theatre, I marvelled again at his ability to wear costume as though it were a second skin. When Richardson appeared in a period play he had the knack of making everyone else look as if they were wearing fancy dress.

Olivier's versatility as an actor makes it difficult to pick out outstanding moments in his long career. If I were forced to choose a handful, they would be drawn from his performances as Archie Rice in *The Entertainer*, as Oedipus in *Oedipus Rex* and as Richard in *Richard III*. When Olivier played Archie Rice, he was able to draw on many of his natural gifts as an actor: his quirky, self-deprecating sense of humour; his depth of emotion; his mobility of face; and all his powers of physical expression. His music hall performance in *The Entertainer* was the fusion of observation, emotion and technique into a completely convincing characterisation. He said himself that Archie Rice was his favourite part.

Then there was that great cry from the blinded Oedipus which echoes in theatrical history. When one considers that he followed this performance with his inimitable, stylised Mr. Puff in Sheridan's *The Critic*, one realises the range of this actor's power. The economy of style and the precision of the effects he made in his first speech remain a highlight of his *Richard III*,

> "Now is the Winter of our discontent
> Made glorious Summer by this sun of York."

The words were spoken syllable by syllable, with a silky, sinister intensity.

Sometimes, a whole scene is photographed by the memory with startling clarity. Such a one was the quarrel scene between Sir Peter and Lady Teazle in *The School for Scandal* which Olivier played with Vivien Leigh, he covering his delight in his young wife with crusty remonstrance - she all grace and provocative charm, a Dresden China figure.

Most great actors have one quality which they have made particularly their own. That quality in Peggy Ashcroft was pathos, a heartbreaking vulnerability. And yet underneath it there was tremendous strength. This was clearly shown when she played Catherine Sloper in *The Heiress*. When she had her revenge on the suitor who had jilted her and she was accused of cruelty, she replied,

> "I have been taught by masters."

The way she said this chilled the blood. There was a mixture of pathos and indestructibility, too, in her performance as Imogen in *Cymbeline*. She was bewitching in the scene when she entered the cave:

144

"Ho! Who's here?
If anything that's civil, speak; if savage
Take or lend. Ho! No answer? Then I'll enter
Best draw my sword: and if mine enemy
But fear the sword, like me, he'll scarcely look on't".

I laughed, but at the same time I wanted to cry.

Later in her career, when she played Winnie in Beckett's *Happy Days*, time had deepened these characteristic qualities. She had, of course, other weapons in her armoury. When she was cold, she could be terrifying. There was an exchange of dialogue in *Hedda Gabler* between herself and Tesman, after they had returned from their honeymoon which I can still hear as clearly as when she spoke it:

**Tesman:**          I was being romantic.

**Hedda** (*idly turning the pages of a paper she is reading*):
          Oh. Is that what you were being.

All my sympathies were with the hapless Tesman at that moment. The boredom in her voice was lethal.

I have already described the powerful effect made by Wolfit's King Lear on everyone who saw it and have singled out the lines which heightened the poignancy for me. In fact, his whole performance, from the time he realised that his reason was slipping,

"O! Let me not be mad, not mad, sweet heaven;
Keep me in temper I would not be mad!"

to the end of the play, was a series of moments which made the throat ache with compassion for the much abused old man.

Alec Guinness, that character actor par excellence, gave an indication of his powers of characterisation early on in his career when he played the part of Herbert Pockett in his own adaptation of *Great Expectations*. There was a luminous vitality about it, he *was* the character. Later on, he was unforgettable as Abel Drugger. This actor has the ability to compel attention even when he is motionless, apparently doing nothing. This was particularly marked in his appearance as Lawrence of Arabia in *Ross*. He walked as an Arab, he sat as an Arab. Even

in repose, his performance was almost hypnotic. I was reminded of it when I saw Albert Finney in *Orphans*. Gagged and tied
to a chair he managed to dominate the stage by the same
magnetism that Alec Guinness had exerted. To my sorrow, I
never saw Edith Evans as Millament - her performance in that
part is legendary.

When one thinks of particular characteristics in relation to
individual actors, the name of Eric Portman springs to mind.
There were two areas of emotion which he made his own: his
power in showing suppressed, but near-hysterical feeling and
his ability to break down emotionally and cry on the stage
without embarrassing an audience.

He demonstrated this in Rattigan's *The Browning Version*.
He played the part of an unpopular master, Andrew Crocker-
Harris, now at the end of his career. He has a heart condition.
Taplow, the boy he has been coaching has given him a book.

**Andrew:**   For me?

**Taplow:**   Yes sir. I've written in it.

What he has written in the book, in Greek, is "God from afar looks
graciously upon a gentle master."

**Andrew** (*His hands are shaking. He lowers the book*)**:**

Taplow, would you be good enough to take that
bottle of medicine, which you so kindly brought
in, and pour me out one dose in a glass which you
will find in the bathroom.

**Taplow:**   Yes sir . . .

He darts out. Andrew breaks down and begins to sob uncon-
trollably. He sits in the chair left of the desk and makes a des-
perate attempt to control himself, but when Taplow comes back
his emotion is still very apparent. Mary Ellis said, in a recent
broadcast, that when she was playing Crocker-Harris' wife,
she used to stand in the wings, night after night, at that point in
the play and marvel at Portman's performance.

As a nation, we have a long tradition of fine acting. Nowadays, it is getting even stronger in depth. Although Peggy
Ashcroft, Olivier and Richardson are dead, and Gielgud is
nearing the end of his career, there is a wealth of talent following

in their footsteps. It has been of absorbing interest to watch this development of younger actors from their earliest appearances to the present day.

Dorothy Tutin's little French Princess in *Henry V* at the Old Vic was a delight, the beginning of a series of sensitive, beautifully judged performances. Renèe Asherson in the same role, this time in Olivier's filmed version of the play, gave equal pleasure. Her scene with Alice, her maid, in which she was trying to master the difficulties of learning English demonstrated how one should move in period costume and was, in fact, one of the highlights of the whole film.

The first time I saw Joan Plowright was as the Cabin Boy in Orson Welle's production of *Moby Dick*. This was an interesting characterisation. However, I was not prepared for the radiance with which she illuminated the closing minutes of Arnold Wesker's *Roots* in the production at the Royal Court Theatre:

"Listen to me . . . mother, Frank . . . I'm beginning on my own two feet. I'm beginning."

It was as if the sun had suddenly come out in a blaze of glory and had lit up the whole auditorium.

Gradually, the memories come closer but these earlier ones are no less vivid than today's. That production of *Roots* was in 1959. Nearly ten years later, Alec McCowen exploded into fame with his performance as Hadrian VII at the Mermaid Theatre. His whole characterisation had a brittle vitality, but the lines which I remember best are those which he shouted through the door at his landlady,

"You can't get manure from a rocking-horse, you rapacious concupiscent female."

Some actors seem to be marked down for stardom at their first appearance; others work steadily through repertory and tours and finally reach the West End. It has been interesting to watch Paul Eddington grow in experience and stature through a series of comedy parts. His furious sense of frustration as the director in Michael Frayn's *Noises Off* was beautifully judged and he has continued to develop his gift for comedy in the television series *Yes Minister* and *Yes Prime Minister*. His particular gift is an ability to judge and time facial reactions. His stardom on stage and television has been well earned.

Judi Dench, on the other hand, always looked like an actress destined for a distinguished future. I was tremendously impressed by her forthright honesty as a performer when I saw her in *The Promise*, early on in her career. She is a generous actress. Then, as now, she put no screen between herself and her audience.

Michael Bryant, too, has always been interesting to watch, from his early appearance as Walter, the German tutor, in *Five Finger Exercise* to his current work at the National Theatre. His technique is now so secure, his acting appears to be so easy, that he is often under-rated. He is probably best described as 'an actor's actor'. Professionals have always realised how good he is. His performance as Enobarbus in Peter Hall's production of *Antony and Cleopatra* was so good that it nearly stole the show.

Another actor who has consistently 'got it right' over the years, is Richard Briers. He is that rarity, a good actor in farce. He brings to his performances an engaging grin, apparent sincerity, the ability to time and to play fast - making his comedy points lightly but firmly. Of the many hours of pleasure he has given, it would be difficult to pick out one particular instant, but one must salute an actor who has learned his job thoroughly, who understands the genre in which he is playing and has always maintained a high level of performance. Now he has extended his range to include tragedy and character parts. Charles Osborne has described his performance as King Lear as making "the tempest in the king's mind as real as the storm outside." He was a fine Malvolio and he brought a breadth and humanity to the part of Bardolph in Kenneth Branagh's film of *Henry V*.

In the 1990s we are lucky to be so rich in acting talent. Some earlier and more recent performances stand out: Samantha Bond as Beatrice in the Renaissance *Much Ado About Nothing*; Tony Britton as Wolsey in Chichester's *Henry VIII*; Rosemary Harris as Dame Laurentia McLachlan in *The Best of Friends*;

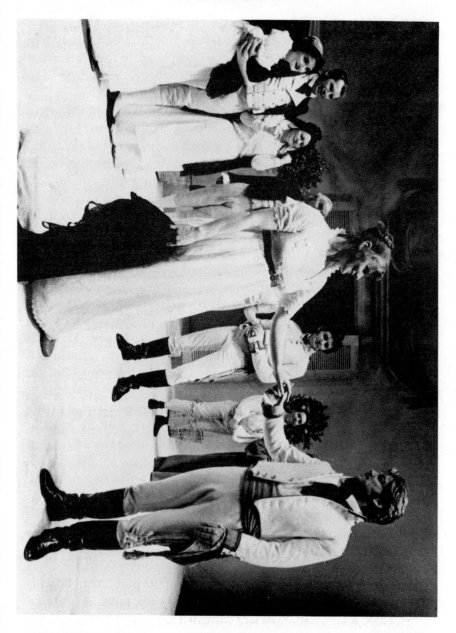

Figure 5: Samantha Bond as Beatrice and Kenneth Branagh as Benedick in *Much Ado About Nothing*. Photograph by Sophie Yauner. By kind permission of the Renaissance Theatre Company.

Nicky Henson as Ford in the Royal Shakespeare Company's production of *The Merry Wives of Windsor*; Rosaleen Linehan in *Dancing at Lughnasa*. And Dennis Quilley as Sir Oliver Surface in *The School for Scandal*; and Nigel Hawthorne as George III in *The Madness of George III* (both at the National).

We have actors of the calibre of Alan Bates, Judi Dench, Michael Gambon, John Gielgud, Derek Jacobi, Robert Lindsay, Ian McKellen, Jonathan Pryce, Vanessa Redgrave, Maggie Smith, Dorothy Tutin and Harriet Walters doing consistently good work - and many more, too numerous to mention.

What of the younger potential leaders of the profession? Kenneth Branagh must be considered to be one of the most promising. When I went to see him in *Henry V* at Stratford, at the invitation of Siôn Probert, a former student who was playing Fluellen, I was remembering Richard Burton's performance of years before and in particular the "Crispin Crispian" speech spoken before Agincourt. Branagh's delivery of the lines in no way eclipsed Burton's, but where I did think that he surpassed him was in the wooing scene with the French Princess. This was done with the lightest touch of humour, with boyish charm and a natural-seeming spontaneity. He achieved the same effect in the film.

I have followed Kenneth Branagh's meteoric rise in the profession since I first saw him in the West End as Judd in *Another Country*. During his Renaissance Company's first season at the Phoenix Theatre it was interesting to observe his approach to three contrasted roles; Touchstone in *As You Like It*; the Prince in *Hamlet*; and Benedick in *Much Ado About Nothing*. Of the three, Benedick was the best-judged - a witty, unselfish performance. He displayed his talent for comic invention as Touchstone. This was a bold, innovative characterisation that succeeded in making the clown's notoriously difficult lines funny, but tended to upset the balance of the play. Although his Hamlet had some powerful emotional moments, at others it revealed an immature lack of control. However, his more recent performance in the part has shown added depth and technical security.

Figure 6: Kenneth Branagh as Benedick and Samantha Bond as Beatrice in *Much Ado About Nothing*. Photograph by Sophie Yauner. By kind permission of the Renaissance Theatre Company.

Branagh has not been helped by the extravagant claims made for him by his admirers. This has been countered by over-harsh criticism, especially from fellow-actors. I am reminded of a remark made to me years ago when I came home from school in tears, saying, "They've been beastly to me because I've won the prize for reading aloud." My mother's comforting comment was that "People only throw stones at trees which are loaded".

There is no denying Branagh's talent: as an actor, director, and a man of the theatre. In the foreword to his autobiography, *Beginning,* he quotes from *As You Like It*:

"I will tell you the beginning and, if it please your ladyships, you may see the end, for the best is yet to do. "

This I believe. If he will undergo the long apprenticeship which is part of the training of a great actor he may well join the illustrious names of the past.

With such a galaxy of acting talent, the future of the theatre should be rosy. But there are insidious forces at work against it. One of these is the influence of television.

We live in an age of instant stardom. An actor has only to appear in a good part in a television series to be referred to as 'a star'. When he appears in his first stage play or pantomime he is often billed above the title. This sudden rise to fame has nothing to do with the dedicated stage actor's slow and sometimes painful learning of his craft. This 'instant star' is all too often faced with instant oblivion when he finds that he is not up to the demands made on him by the leading part in a stage play.

So far I have been concentrating on great acting in plays. It may also be found in such diverse milieux as opera, revue and music hall. I saw the opera-singer Mariano Stabile give a magnificent acting performance as Doctor Malatesta in *Don Pasquale* and who will ever forget Sid Field in his famous golfing sketch or as Slasher Green? Later he was a great success as the leading character in *Harvey.*

One of the most impressive illustrations of the way an artist can hold an audience in the palm of his hand was given by Maurice Chevalier in his one-man show. Even towards the end of his career, his domination was remarkable. He achieved it by the magnetism of his personality and by the brilliance of his technique. He himself admitted that he did not have a great singing voice and was no Fred Astaire. But he was a dedicated worker. He revealed in his autobiography his view of his work:

"an artist carries on throughout his life a mysterious, uninterrupted conversation with his public."

Revue has often been the nursery of performers. Four different talents were reared in *Beyond the Fringe*. It was full of hilarious moments and the one I remember best occurred at the end of a parody of a Shakespearean history play. After one of the characters, the Earl of Worcester had taken "an unconscionable time dying", he was given a final tribute in the words "O saucy Worcester".

One of the finest pieces of character acting I have seen came from the music hall artist, the male impersonator, Hetty King. In the last days of the old Metropolitan Theatre in Edgeware Road there was a series of shows put on which featured some of the stars of the great days of music hall. It was at the Met. that I saw Hetty King as an old Sailor ("Every nice girl loves a sailor") and as a West End toff. As she was then in her seventies, what we were privileged to see was the distillation of a lifetime's work in two short sketches. Her stage business had been honed to a fine art - the lighting of the old salt's pipe, the tamping down of the tobacco in the bowl, the lighting up, the throwing away of the match and catching it on her heel on its way down. I sat through her second-house performance just to see that moment again. Unerringly the match hit the heel.

I thought of the descriptions of two other examples of such precision. One was Harold Hobson's account of the way Ralph Lynn dropped his monocle on a key word to point a line in the middle of an air raid. The other was Julie Harris' detailed recollection of some stage business Olivier used as Mr. Puff:

"I used to watch Sir Laurence when he played Mr. Puff in *The Critic*. To the identical syllable, in each performance, he would take off his hat, take out the hatpin and stab the hat with the hatpin. He didn't vary a hair's breadth from performance to performance, yet it was always funny and always astonishing."

Hetty King, in her other character of a drunken toff, judged her zig-zag staggering walk from one side of the stage to the other (where she just managed to catch the proscenium arch for support), with the same apparently artless skill. This sketch demonstrated how to present drunkenness on the stage without either over- or under-doing it and was rapturously received by the audience.

One of the most fascinating things about studying actors in performance is to listen to the individual timbre of their voices. The dictionary definition of timbre is interesting. It is defined as the, "characteristic quality of sounds produced by each particular voice or instrument, depending on the number and character of the overtones."

Paul Scofield's voice has an unusually distinctive timbre. Over the years I can still hear the way he spoke these lines from John Osborne's *The Hotel in Amsterdam*:

**Laurie:**    To me . . . you have always been the most dashing . . . romantic . . . friendly . . . playful . . . loving . . . impetuous . . . larky . . . fearful . . . detached . . . constant . . . woman I have ever met . . . and I love you . . . I don't know how else one says it . . . one shouldn't . . . and I've always thought you felt . . . perhaps . . . the same about me.

**Annie:**    I do.

**Laurie:**    When we are all away - you are never out of my heart.

He separated the words as indicated in the text and delivered them with grave simplicity. It was an intensely moving scene. Paul Scofield speaks the English language unlike any other actor, Kenneth Tynan once described him as being "sweetly eccentric."

The same is even truer of Donald Sinden. As a specialist teacher of voice and speech I must admit to being somewhat shaken by his idiosyncratic treatment of vowels and consonants. He, like Nöel Coward, pronounces English in a style peculiar to himself. However, this style came into its own when he played Sir Percy Blakeney in *The Scarlet Pimpernel*. He shaded in the difference beautifully between the voice of foppish Sir Percy and that of the intrepid Scarlet Pimpernel.

# Drama Critics and Adjudicators

Different people respond in different ways to great acting. One drama critic told me that he knew he was watching a great performance, "by the pricking of my thumbs". Another felt the hairs rising on the back of his neck. People usually cannot analyse why they know that they are watching great acting; the rationale comes afterwards.

Drama critics and adjudicators are often asked if the job they are doing spoils their enjoyment of the play. In my experience, if the play is done well the sense of enjoyment is heightened. One is aware of the technical problems of a particular genre being solved, or of a particularly difficult emotional scene being brought off successfully. If the play is badly done, critics and adjudicators suffer more than the average audience member, because they are more aware of what is going wrong on the stage. Some shows can seem interminable. On the whole, I enjoy adjudicating at amateur festivals. But it is a demanding, difficult job, calling for sustained concentration. Along with the responsibility of recognising talent there is the onerous job of having to explain why some acting is bad.

In my off-duty theatregoing, I have the added pleasure of knowing that I do not have to get up on the stage to talk about the show. This is even greater when I am at an amateur production which someone else is adjudicating, because I am inwardly thankful that it's their job and not mine tonight - I can relax!

The former drama critic of *The Sunday Times*, James Agate, composed an epitaph for himself:

"Though
In his declining years
He used the words
*Great, first-class, pre-eminent*
Indiscriminately
Like everybody else
James Agate
At his unclouded best
Allowed no second-rate player
To get past him."

James Agate was trenchant in his remarks about some critics of his day,

"All around me young critics, even in the theatre, are being kind to players who, in the days before the film existed, would have been told to get off the boards and go and learn their job."

One is uncomfortably aware, looking at the West End today, that if the word 'television' were substituted for 'film', this remark still has some application.

## Threats to the Theatre

As well as the effect of television's 'instant stardom' on the theatre, there is the threat to the actor of the increased use of technology. The ears of audiences are being deafened by amplified sound. Microphones are in use in theatres where formerly actors were able to project their voices so that they were heard in every part of the auditorium. Players learn to depend on them, with the result that when microphones are switched off audiences frequently complain that they cannot hear the words.

Some sound-men are becoming aware of this threat. John Leonard, for example, of the RSC has this to say,

"New technology is fine when we are able to use it to our advantage, but when we allow it to dictate our attitudes and, in some cases, to replace creativity and skill, then is the time to be wary."

That time has now arrived. Even more attention should be given during an actor's training to the development of his voice and speech. Then we might start to limit the use of the ubiquitous microphone.

In addition to the effect of television and advanced technology on the theatre we now see a new threat - the increasing domination of musicals in the West End. A list of London theatre attendances for 1990 confirms this in a startling way. While 58,490 seats were sold for traditional and modern musicals, the figure for plays (including modern drama, classical plays, comedies and thrillers) was 37,300. The facts speak for themselves.

# *Epilogue*

# *The Shape of Things to Come*

"The lyf so short, the craft so long to lerne"
*Chaucer*

In many ways, today's young actors have advanced immeasurably in their range of skills. They are trained to move, dance, sing, tumble, juggle and fence. They are encouraged to explore texts in depth through improvisation, discussion and research. They are able to think for themselves: they refuse to be typecast and are not afraid to take risks and to experiment. They do, however, lack a sense of history - even the history of their own profession. It is not uncommon to hear drama students asking such questions as 'Who was Henry Irving?' or 'Ellen Terry - who was she?'

We live in an arrogant age. Many people feel that in the arts, nothing which happened before the First World War is of any importance. In a recent letter to the press the writer dismissed what he called,

"The accretion of myth, legend and fairytale, the elaborate conceits of bygone days,"

as having no value. Of course, each age must create its own legends, styles, attitudes. Of course, we need to experiment, to view things freshly. T. S. Eliot expressed this need:

"For last years' words belong to last years' language
And next years' words await another voice."

But today's young actors can surely learn from what is best in the past and, at the same time, make their own contribution to the future.

## Would-be Actors

Every year, thousands of would-be actors apply for an audition to one or more of the mushrooming drama schools. Since the *Fame* series appeared on television the number of aspiring actors has increased. Many of them have little idea of what going on the stage involves. Some are not clear as to what their motive is, and would find difficulty in answering the following questions. 'Do you want to be an actor, or do you just want to be famous?' 'Would you be miserable doing anything else?' 'What contribution do you think you have to offer, should you enter the profession?' 'What do you think an actor's life is like?'

A young girl arrived on my doorstep the other day and asked to be coached for an audition. As she had not prepared anything, I asked her to read a speech. She was not a good sight-reader but this, in itself, was not a serious drawback. Many good actors do not read well at sight. We went through the speech again together, analysing the meaning, the character's motive, the style.

I then put the speech in the context of the whole play and we talked about the shape of the speech, where the climax came and so on. This breakdown took an hour, and at the end she said, "Oh, isn't it hard work!" She was amazed, even disillusioned.

Certainly she was not prepared to undergo the blood, toil, tears and sweat which go into the making of an actor.

Some students think that a drama coach has only to blow a magic powder over them and, hey-presto, their voice will become well produced and their speech distinct. I am sometimes asked, 'How long will it take to cure my nasal voice/my hissing 'S' sound/my weak 'R' sound?' The answer is that it depends on the student. A person needs to be strongly motivated, to have a good ear, to be willing to work patiently and conscientiously over a period of time to achieve results. Voice and speech faults do not disappear overnight. Motivation is all-important. Some actors, when they find that they can get plenty of work, do not attempt to correct quite glaring vocal and speech faults because they think they do not matter.

## The 'Natural'

There is such a thing as a 'natural', someone who intuitively seems to know it all and has never thought about technique. This natural talent is not confined to the professional theatre. I once adjudicated at a drama festival in East Anglia where an elderly lady, in a one-act play, gave a brilliant performance - touching, controlled, fully communicated. When I met the cast afterwards, I congratulated her and asked her if in her earlier days she had ever thought of going into the acting profession. She looked surprised and then said mildly, "How funny, that was what the gentleman who came last year asked me." Naturals, however, are few and far between. The majority of us have to work at mastering our technique.

## Play-going

The theatre can be exciting, surprising, stimulating and provocative in all its aspects, whether one is a playwright, director, actor, designer, stage manager or spectator. The playgoer never knows when he is going to glimpse that moment of greatness and be made aware that something which is supremely difficult to do is being done with apparent ease. I come back to Torvill and Dean, whose artistry sparked off this attempt to describe the actor's art and craft.

I have not, of course, given an exhaustive list of the great moments that I have experienced in my theatregoing life - human memory is fallible. And I have not included foreign actors playing in their own language, for example: Edwige Feuillère and the Russian Gribov whose performance in the Moscow Arts Theatre's production of *The Cherry Orchard* was a *tour de force*.

Finally, the whole book is not so much a tribute to individual performances and moments of unforgettable contact between actor and audience, but to the art and craft of acting itself.

# Index of Actors, Authors and Texts

164

# Auditioning: A Practical Guide

*Auditioning* meets two specific needs: it helps would-be actors who have applied for auditions at drama schools; and it is of use to drama students who are looking for suitable material to have in their repertoire when they go into the profession. Rona Laurie gives advice on the choice and presentation of suitable material for auditions. There are two speeches with detailed instructions on performance. A list of suggested speeches for women and for men auditioning for schools and for the profession: straight and serious speeches, comedy, character and Shakespeare excerpts; and material for children's theatre auditions.

"It equips young people to cope with a situation for which there is rarely adequate guidance and gives a thoroughly honest picture of the perils and possibilities of professional auditions. There is sound advice on the approach and preparation, the choice of material and the actual moment of performance." - *Speech and Drama*

"one of our most experienced teachers and adjudicators presents here a handy guide to a thorny problem, even for professional actors. As well as detailing what one should wear and how one conducts oneself - essential for would-be actors - the book also contains a lengthy list of suitable audition pieces." - *The Stage*

**64pages.**                                          **ISBN: 0 85643 585 5**

# Festivals and Adjudication

Rona Laurie's wide experience as a festival speech and drama adjudicator, makes this book a *must* for anyone involved in drama or music festivals. *Organisers* will find descriptions of the types of festival. *Adjudicators* will be introduced to their art. *Competitors* will find guidance on selection and presentation of material. And *audiences* will learn to compare their judgements with the judges'. All will enjoy a rich supply of anecdotes.

**150 pages.**                                        **ISBN: 0 273 25257 7**

## J. Garnet Miller Limited

# J. Garnet Miller Limited

Publisher of plays and theatre books. Established 1953.

## Theatre Books:

*Acting Up! - An Innovative Approach to Creative Drama*
*Adaptable Stage Costume for Women*
*Auditioning: a Practical Guide*
*Composers and their Times - Bach and Schubert*
*Design for Movement*
*Drama Improvised*
*Festivals and Adjudication*
*Improvisation: Project and Practice*
*Playing Period Plays*
*The Producer and the Actor*
*Stage Fights*
*Stage Management and Theatrecraft*

## New Titles:

*Choreographing the Stage Musical*
*The Musical Director in the Amateur Theatre*
*Musicals: the Guide to Amateur Production*

Full details of all our theatre books
and plays can be obtained from

**J. Garnet Miller Limited**